UNIVERSITY
STUDENT
HANDBOOK

"I felt like you were writing about my own experience when I arrived in the UK 17 years ago! Thank you for writing this book for the Chinese students - it's exactly what they need."

Yiyun Ling
Careers Practitioner

"A comprehensive book that will really help many Chinese international students find their footing when studying in the UK. This guide is so useful as it covers more than just careers but also aids in personal development to help students gain insights and build their self-confidence over time."

Lisa Chow
Careers Consultant for ICMA Centre
Henley Business School, University of Reading

UNIVERSITY STUDENT HANDBOOK

FROM CHINA TO THE UK

An essential guide for students
from China going to UK universities.
How to have a successful experience
and get a head start in
your career.

SUZANNA TAN

BROWN
DOG
BOOKS

Published under licence by Brown Dog Books and
The Self-Publishing Partnership, 7 Green Park Station, Bath BA1 1JB

www.selfpublishingpartnership.co.uk

ISBN printed book: 978-1-83952-202-4
ISBN e-book: 978-1-83952-203-1

Cover design by Kevin Rylands
Internal design by Andrew Easton

Printed and bound in the UK

This book is printed on FSC certified paper

DEDICATED TO THE PARENTS
OF THE STUDENTS
I'VE WRITTEN THIS BOOK FOR

Contents

Foreword

"I'm so impressed with you. You've demonstrated outstanding communication skills in two different languages, even while working under pressure and with teammates you've never met. You aren't afraid to put yourself forward for a task, even when you are slightly apprehensive about not having all of the facts or sufficient time to think things through. You work well in a team by demonstrating leadership and taking charge when needed. We definitely want to offer you the job and are absolutely thrilled to hopefully have you join our global team."

Are these the words (or similar words) you'd like to hear after undertaking your degree in the UK?

Are you worried you can't demonstrate the skills wanted by future employers?

Are you excited to move abroad to experience a new culture but worried you won't make new friends or be able to speak English as well as your non-Chinese classmates?

If any of these words ring true to you, then you've already proven how astute you are by opening this book!

I've been working in Higher Education since 2012, after being in the private sector for nearly two decades, mostly in Talent Acquisition and Learning & Development. I started working at universities because I saw the opportunity to help bridge the gap between what employers really look for and what students leave university with. Please don't get me wrong, I think universities have always done an excellent job of preparing students. The larger issue, in my opinion, was the fact that employer job descriptions asked for every skill under the sun and students often didn't know which skills to emphasise in applications and interviews.

Often I get told, "You lead a university careers team, and your team's job is to check CVs and applications". Yes, that is certainly part of it, but ultimately our job is preparing students for the constantly changing world of work. It's not just about selling yourself effectively in your CV or interview, it's about developing skills that allow you to shine and perform at a high level, whether you want a job or your own business. Internships and work experience are certainly examples of where you can develop and demonstrate skills but you should also have examples from academic endeavours and volunteering.

I am extremely fortunate to lead a talented and award-winning business school careers team. Between us we have over 50 years of experience working with international students, mostly from China. The extra layer of our challenge is helping those students navigate a new environment with a completely different culture than they are used to. With that being said, our biggest challenge is lack of time. It takes students time to acclimate to the environment, get used to local customs, keep up with rigorous coursework, etc. Quite often, students wait until the end of the year to engage with our team and that's simply too late.

That is where Suzanna Tan and this book comes in!

Suzanna was recommended to me through a colleague who was aware our team was short-handed during our busiest time of the year. It was obvious Suzanna could help our students, not just because of her years of corporate and coaching experience, and her academic and professional credentials. It only took a short conversation with Suzanna for me to realise her real value is her ability to reflect and use all her old and new knowledge, skills and experience to address the root causes of why students from China sometimes struggle. Suzanna has the unique ability to look at it holistically. She takes it back to basics which I think really helps students, not just for their careers, but crucially for their personal growth too.

I feel this book is not so much a self-help book as it is a handbook on how to approach your study abroad. Whether you are a postgraduate or undergraduate student, it is my opinion that if you follow Suzanna's advice, you will put yourself in a better position to succeed. Make no mistake though, it will be difficult. You will arrive wanting to improve your English but if you aren't careful, you'll find yourself speaking more Mandarin than English depending on your peer network. You will have to work to create a diverse circle of friends as Suzanna details well in this book. Suzanna not only simplifies how you can maximise your experiences in the UK, she helps you stand out in the crowded graduate market. I have no doubt that if you do most of what she suggests, you will dramatically improve both your UK experience and your career prospects.

I highly recommend this book as I'm confident you will learn a lot from it, but only you will determine your success. Some of Suzanna's suggestions are those I tell to hundreds of students each year but only a few follow through. I assume you are reading this book because you want to prosper in your career, personal life, or both. The ball is in your court, please take Suzanna's tips and advice and run with them. If you do, I am confident you will look back a few years into your career and say, "I'm really glad I read that book!"

Tripp Martin
Head of Careers in Business
Birmingham Business School
University of Birmingham, UK

Introduction

When you come from China to study in the UK you may have expectations of getting a good degree, meeting different friends, experiencing UK life, securing a job or laying the foundations for a successful career. So why do some students struggle and feel isolated during university life, and return to China a little more disillusioned than when they came to the UK?

The challenges you may face when you get to the UK can influence your overall well-being and capability to thrive in the new environment. This in turn can impact your personal growth and ability to prepare for your career. Thus, being aware of and prepared for the expected and unexpected will enable you to navigate through to make the most of all the opportunities open to you.

This book is based on experiences of hundreds of students from China studying at UK universities, research with careers experts at UK universities, and what employers in the UK and China look for. It highlights what some students may experience and offers suggestions to guide you through your own university journey. Whether you have chosen a UK university to expand your personal growth or to enhance your career prospects, this book is a comprehensive handbook to help you have a great experience.

The student stories in this book are not based on any particular students, but have been inspired by many students whom I and other career practitioners have had the pleasure of engaging with. All names and stories shared are fictional and only used to help you understand and reflect on the experiences and what can be done to address them. The stories that start each chapter were constructed to illustrate situations students can sometimes find themselves in which are relevant to the chapter's topic. Although I have presented many issues highlighted in the stories, not every student faces every issue. Throughout the chapters I include short anecdotes which may have been inspired by students, but have been adapted to bring to life the points I am making.

How to use this book

Coming to study at university in the UK means different things to different students. Whatever your reasons, they will probably fall into the categories of personal growth or career preparation. Your priority may be to have a great social experience taking advantage of the exciting new environment, or it may be to get a good degree or to gain experience to help your career. I believe you can have it all. It may take some focus and planning, and there may be times when you have to push yourself outside your comfort zone. Whether you are in the UK for an undergraduate or postgraduate degree, there are things you can do to achieve what you want and more.

You will encounter a very steep learning curve when you come to the UK, so the ideal time to read this book is at least six months before you go to the UK. This will help you start preparing and be prepared for what's to come. You can also use the information in each chapter during your time in the UK.

- Part 1 focuses on your *personal growth* to help you settle into UK university life.
- Part 2 focuses on *career preparation* to help you get ready for your career.

Chapter 1 is the important aspect of improving your English

fluency, because this lays the foundations for your UK university experience. Chapters 2 and 3 are essential to support your well-being and settling in quickly. Chapters 4, 5 and 6 support you to develop broader foundations for a successful future career. Then Chapters 7, 8 and 9 are additional sources of guidance you can use to help your career journey. You may wish to read the whole book, or choose chapters most relevant to you, or read the summary at the end of each chapter referring back to the whole chapter if it resonates.

I cannot promise that you will get your dream job or have a successful business. What I can do is show you how to have a fully rounded UK university experience, which I hope provides you with happy memories and a platform to build a fulfilling and successful career.

I wish you all the best and hope this book makes your journey much easier.

Part 1
PERSONAL GROWTH

Chapter 1

IMPROVING YOUR ENGLISH FLUENCY

Zhang Wei was pleased he passed his IELTs English language test with 7.0, as his UK university only asked for 6.5. However, at Heathrow Airport he struggled to understand the Border Force officer at Immigration and she struggled to understand him. Zhang Wei felt embarrassed and tongue-tied as he tried to answer her questions. His early experience of conversing in English knocked his confidence.

During Freshers' Week he joined the Chinese Society and hoped to join other clubs to mix with English-speaking students, but felt awkward approaching them as they were talking so quickly and he couldn't understand them so didn't go back. He couldn't keep up with what his lecturers said, so recorded them and listened again to the lectures, diligently writing notes. He read through the extensive reading lists, but when writing his first assignment he didn't know how to bring it all together. He spent most of his time studying, trying to keep up and pass his modules with little time for other activities. When he took breaks he was with other students from China as his halls were made up of international students and everyone spoke Mandarin.

After his first year he reflected on how the year had gone and realised he had not had the university experience he hoped for and, although his reading and writing had improved, he felt he had not practised his English conversational skills. In his second year he made himself join clubs and societies he was interested in, and got himself a voluntary job showing new students around the university. He found himself mentoring the new Chinese students to help them settle in, making sure he spoke in English, encouraging them to do so, too.

Passing your IELTs (International English Language Testing System) test allows you to demonstrate you have the basic level of English proficiency to study at university, but these are just minimum standards. Having a higher level of English fluency before you arrive in the UK will give you a good start.

How to prepare before going to university in the UK

Some students attend intensive English language classes in China or the UK during the summer before their degree starts. These are usually tailored to help you prepare for studying in English. In the UK specialist language schools offer a range of levels of English language classes tailored for international students. The associated course and living costs vary according to the school and city they are located in. English language classes are sometimes offered by universities specifically for improving English language skills before your degree starts. Some universities offer these classes as a prerequisite for students with conditional offers who failed their IELTS. Look at your university to see what the options are.

If you don't attend additional English classes you can improve your fluency using some of the ideas in this chapter. Whilst studying for English language tests you will be familiar with the four different skills needed to master a language: Reading, Writing, Listening and Speaking.

Reading

Reading is not just about being able to read the words; it's about comprehending what you read. The words you read make up the messages or the story being told. Comprehension is key to ensure you can understand and debate what you read. You already have fluency in reading and comprehending Chinese which enables you to study effectively in Chinese. Similarly, reading fluency in English is core to being able to study effectively in English.

Students often use translation tools to convert texts from English into Chinese. However, this can be inefficient because it is time-consuming and underlying messages can be lost in translation. With extensive literature reading lists in academic styles of writing, there are sometimes no direct words to translate and grammar further complicates translations, resulting in them not making sense.

How to improve your reading fluency

The majority of course modules include a broad range of reading so you can demonstrate your ability to collate information to inform your ideas. Here are some ideas of what you can do to improve your reading fluency.

Read books in English. Whether you enjoy reading science fiction, biographies, short stories or romance novels, it doesn't matter. Get used to the flow of words, storylines, what the author is telling you, descriptions of the scenes and situations, and where the story takes you. You can read books you have already read in Chinese. If you are interested in something, you will be more likely to read it. Before you know it you will have the confidence and capability to understand what you read. This in turn will provide you with increased ability to read and understand academic texts. Some students find comparative reading useful where a book has both English and Chinese because they can compare direct word and sentence translations.

Read a broad range of news stories. Newspapers or press stories online on current affairs are useful and easy ways of accessing reading to improve your reading comprehension and range of vocabulary. By exposing yourself to different writing styles, you start understanding how different people communicate in different ways.

Read academic literature in your chosen area of study. You can request the reading list for your modules in advance of your course or look these up online. Even if you read related academic literature not on the list, it won't be a waste of time because extensive reading of this type of literature will improve your comprehension of academic texts, and provide a broad range of knowledge to draw on throughout your modules.

Read your university website. This is a useful way of looking at what your university has to offer or what you need to know before you attend. Some universities provide specific sections for international students, careers information, course information, and lots more. It's a great way to practise reading English whilst finding out more about what you need to know before you go to your university.

Read anything that interests you in English. Focus on reading things you are interested in and what you may normally read in Chinese. Don't pick anything too difficult as it may discourage you.

Writing

The ability to write fluently is also important when studying in the UK. Writing using the correct grammar and vocabulary can be difficult, especially when trying to articulate your thoughts in an academic style at the same time. Students with English as their first language may also struggle to write in an academic style, so for someone who has English as a second or even third language, the challenge is greater.

When writing an assignment, an option is to write your first draft freely so you can fully express what you want to say. At this stage you don't have to worry about grammar, vocabulary or spelling. By letting your thoughts flow, you get everything down first. The next step would be to organise your writing so it makes sense and is structured correctly according to what your assignment asks for. Once you have done that, you can focus on correcting grammar, vocabulary and spelling. For spelling and vocabulary, a dictionary and thesaurus are useful tools. Your university may have workshops to help with writing assignments and dissertations.

How to improve your writing fluency

Write a daily journal in English. This helps you get into the habit of writing your thoughts freely. By doing this regularly you start to get quicker and better at writing. Check your grammar, vocabulary and spelling, too. The more you do this, the more practice you get, and your free writing will get easier.

Practise writing sentences. You can start writing short, simple sentences and then elaborate the sentence in steps so it has more depth and meaning. It could go something like this:

- *I felt happy today.*
- *I felt happy today because I had some spare time.*
- *I had some spare time today and I was happy reading my new book.*
- *I realised I felt happy today because I had spare time to read the book that I have been meaning to read for a few months.*

Translate text from Chinese into English. You can choose any type of text to translate, perhaps something already translated. You can then compare your translation with it. This will help you understand how the same sentence can be said in both English and Chinese.

Ask someone to check your writing. By asking for feedback on your writing, this helps you see mistakes you are not aware of. Your peers or tutors can help you with this, and you can help your peers by reviewing their writing as well.

Text message others in English. Texting is a useful way to practise spontaneous conversation and will improve your writing skills. Perhaps you can message your friends in English. The grammar doesn't have to be perfect when you have a conversation via text message. It's more about building your confidence in having a conversation which will in turn improve spontaneity and your writing skills. Language exchange partners link language learners up and can link you up with someone who wants to learn Chinese. Some have apps where you can text message your language partner.

Listening

During your English lessons in China, you will hear English spoken clearly and slowly. However, in the UK you will hear English spoken quickly and in a broad range of regional and international accents, which may make it difficult for you to understand. To further complicate this, everyday conversations don't always demonstrate correct grammar and may include slang words or phrases. Socially spoken English is also different to conversations in the workplace where there may be different company or industry-specific words which are unfamiliar to people who do not work there.

How to improve your listening fluency
Watch English movies with Chinese subtitles. Focusing on watching films set in the UK with Chinese subtitles can help you practise listening to English being spoken whilst looking at the subtitles when you need to.

Watch English movies with English subtitles. This time only use English subtitles so you can practise listening to English being spoken whilst looking at the English subtitles. This helps to improve listening and reading at the same time.

Watch English films without subtitles. If you watch English films with no subtitles, it encourages you to listen more to understand what is happening. Films are a great way of practising listening, because the acting helps you understand the storyline.

Watch anything in English. This helps you practise hearing different accents you may come across in the UK. Choose what interests you such as comedy, news, soap operas, or dramas such as a historical drama, detective or murder series. They also provide you with some understanding of social culture in the UK.

Practise active listening. Active listening is being fully present in the moment and listening to what someone is saying. When you listen to someone speak English, notice what is being said, how it is being said and the meaning behind it. Don't be distracted by anything else, such as what you think the person is going to say, otherwise you will lose focus and concentration. If Zhang Wei had practised active listening during his lectures, he may have understood more of what was being said and not needed to listen to recordings again, saving him time.

Listen to music in English. Listening to music with English lyrics can enhance your comprehension, grammar, range of vocabulary and pronunciation. The lyrics can expose you to new words and phrases which may include local slang or common sayings.

Listen to a podcast in English. Find podcasts by people or on topics that interest you. They come in different lengths, and starting with shorter ones will make it easier for you to focus. Longer ones could be listened to in the background as you are doing another activity such as exercising or cooking.

Listen to an audiobook in English. Audiobooks in English provide a relaxing way to practise listening in English. Like with podcasts, books can be listened to in the background.

Speaking

Speaking is what many students find most difficult out of the four elements of learning a new language. This is because speaking requires you to think and convey what you want to say immediately. This can put pressure on you to come up with the correct vocabulary and grammar. There are times when correct vocabulary and grammar are important, such as in examinations or interviews; however, during daily conversations, people are more flexible and excuse the use of incorrect grammar.

One student spent time volunteering at a library which helped improve his English fluency. By having to deal with his manager, colleagues and the general public, he had to speak a lot. After three months his English was more fluent, he no longer paused to think of how to construct his sentences or choose his words, and he talked more naturally. When he first came to the UK he worried more about grammar and vocabulary which made him shy speaking English. Now he realised language was just a tool and it was important for people to understand him, rather than the words or grammar he used. He was no longer bothered about his accent because he felt confident people could understand him.

How to improve your speaking fluency

Don't worry about your accent. Some students may worry about their accent when speaking English; however, this really does not matter. Most people in the UK also have a regional accent and international students have accents.

Shadowing. Copying what someone says is shadowing. It helps with muscle memory because the more you mimic accents, words and sentences, the easier it is to put a sentence together. There are apps for this or you can use a recording of someone speaking English where you can easily stop and rewind the sentences. Play a short audio clip and then copy it by saying the same section out loud in real time. You can repeat the audio clip and speak at the same time as well.

Use a language application. Apps are a useful way of deepening your English learning and complementing your English lessons. You can imitate what the app tells you to repeat and it's a great way of improving intonation and pronunciation.

Buddy up. Find another student who is proficient in English who wants to practise their Mandarin and help each other. Virtual chats alternating between Mandarin and English each time will improve both of your language skills and you can develop a great friendship. Again, language exchange partners can help you with this.

Keep an audio journal in English. Similar to writing a journal in English, recording a journal in English can help improve your speaking. Talking about the things you have done also gives you practise with articulating everyday conversations. It can be rewarding listening back to past recordings and hearing how much you've improved.

Consciously think in English. Although this can be difficult at first, making a conscious effort to think in English will help with fluency. Through practice, you will find words come quicker and you won't need to translate in your head as you speak, enabling you to communicate quicker and more fluently.

Speak English whenever you can. Many students from China feel they don't have opportunities to practise English in the UK because their social circles are mainly Chinese. It's easy and natural to fall back to speaking Mandarin, so finding opportunities to be with students who are not from China is helpful. This can be done by joining clubs or societies to meet a broader range of students. It may be a little outside your comfort zone to attend these groups, but you will find other people are usually welcoming, especially if you go on your own and make the effort to introduce yourself.

Sing in English. If you enjoy music with English lyrics, singing along can be an effective way of improving your speaking. Similar to listening, you will learn new words and phrases. Karaoke can be a fun way to practise this.

Summary – Why English fluency is beneficial

The university requirements are the minimum standards expected for you to do their course, but in reality it's advantageous for you to be more fluent in your Reading, Writing, Listening and Speaking. Getting fluent in English before coming to the UK is the most worthwhile thing you can do. If you are already in the UK, you can also use the ideas in this chapter to continue improving your English. A good level of English fluency supports every element of your UK life because it helps with your personal growth and development, impacts your ability to study more effectively, socialise with other students, and helps with your career development.

Chapter 2

SETTLING INTO UK UNIVERSITY LIFE

Wang Yan was excited to go to the UK for university. Her mother packed her bags with dried sausages, scallops, mushrooms, herbal soup ingredients, instant noodles, and bottles of soya sauce and sesame oil, as well as a small rice cooker and slow cooker to boil soup. At Heathrow Airport, she was embarrassed as a Customs officer checked her luggage, confiscating her dried sausages and instant noodles containing meat products. A few days after she arrived at university, she found a local Chinese food shop stocking all the ingredients and cooking equipment she had carried in from China and wished she had packed more clothes instead.

She found the weather frustrating: one minute it was raining, the next the sun shone. During the second week she felt extremely homesick, missing her mother's cooking and the familiarity of her home. She felt lonely confined to her bedroom at night. Despite having lots of Chinese friends from her halls and course, she started to feel isolated from the world outside from where she lived and studied. Although she found it easier staying in, cooking and eating in the kitchen with her new Chinese friends, she was determined to try to meet other people from different countries. She plucked up the courage and went with a friend to some social events and signed up for day trips organised by the Student Union. She enjoyed the pub crawls, even though she didn't drink alcohol, she found it fun visiting the different pubs. The day trips gave her a chance to go to places she wouldn't have visited, such as walking in the Lake District.

You may have great expectations of what university life in the UK will be like and will want to make the most out of this experience to have an amazing time. All students appreciate university life will be different to being at home and a little shock to the system is normal. Expectations before you come can be different to reality and may take a little while to get used to. In the UK, you may face being in an unfamiliar society with a different way of life, and people around you will have different attitudes or behaviours you are not used to. It's perfectly normal to experience this, and to help you settle in quickly, it's important to be aware and prepared for some of the cultural differences. In this chapter I share some common themes that students from China found surprised them during their first few weeks at UK universities. Hopefully these can help you to prepare or they may already resonate if you have already started studying in the UK.

Accommodation

Halls full of Chinese students. Most students from China find the university has allocated them in accommodation together. This may be a surprise for students because they expected to meet people from different countries, but it also helps students settle in as there is a natural affinity being together.

Quality of accommodation. The quality of accommodation can be variable and may not look like photos you saw when choosing your room. Most now have en suite facilities, but I had a student finding it difficult as she had chosen a room with shared bathroom, shower and toilets. Sharing with others is not always easy, but you will soon get into a routine alongside your other flatmates as you all start to work around each other on when to use the facilities.

Indoor etiquette. In the UK, people generally don't remove shoes before entering inside. One student was horrified when her non-Chinese flatmate came into her room with her shoes on. If this happens, explain politely to your friends that it's what you are used to or even put a small sign up in advance to ask them to kindly remove their shoes.

Adaptors. Electrical equipment you bring from China must be used with a UK plug adapter to be used safely in the UK. You may wish to bring a few adapters to use in your bedroom and kitchen.

Food

Supermarkets. Getting used to different supermarkets can be hard at first, especially knowing how items are priced and product types available. Many students have tried the supermarket's Chinese pre-made food which they have found not quite to their taste – although one particular student was delighted to find Peking duck and pancakes at her local supermarket. It amused her as she had never eaten it in China, yet it was comforting and made her feel at home.

Food in the UK. Due to the multicultural society in the UK a broad range of food is available. University food outlets cater for different food tastes and include a choice of British food such as fried breakfasts, jacket potatoes and pies. Traditional British cuisine can be found in restaurants, cafes and pubs, offering food such as traditional roasts of oven-roasted meats of chicken, pork, beef and lamb served with vegetables, potatoes and gravy. There will also be international variants such as Italian pastas and pizzas, Indian curries or Chinese stir-fry dishes. Chinese students I've spoken to had surprisingly steered away from British food; the few who had tried mentioned fish and chips and breakfasts being delicious but a bit too oily and sandwiches too dry and cold, and some found the food to be a bit heaty, especially after eating too many baked pies and deep-fried food.

Chinese speciality shops. Chinese supermarkets and grocery stores are usually located near universities. They stock Chinese cooking equipment and ingredients such as century and salted eggs, dried ingredients such as mushrooms, scallops, shrimps, squid, sausages and belly pork. So save your luggage space and don't run the risk of getting food items confiscated at the airport. You can also find Chinese vegetables such as bak choi, Chinese spinach, kailan, lotus root and Chinese chives (do not confuse these with unbudded daffodils which look similar and are poisonous). Before you come, search online for Chinese stores local to your university. If there aren't any, your local supermarkets will stock some Chinese ingredients or you can order them online.

Chinese restaurants and takeaways. You can find Chinese restaurants and takeaways close to university and in the town centre. Some cater to the different regional tastes of Chinese customers and some more to the Western palette. You can usually gauge this by looking at the types of customers they have.

Cooking. Many students wish they had learned to cook favourite dishes from their parents. It's fun cooking with other students, and some have loved learning to cook favourite recipes and experimenting with new ones. Grouping together by taking turns to cook for one another can save money and time. For health and safety reasons and under accommodation regulations, do not cook in your bedroom: I've heard of one student consistently cooking in his bedroom and he was eventually evicted from his hall.

Tap water. It is safe to drink water from the cold water tap in the UK. However, it is not safe to consume water from the hot water tap, and using it for cooking or boiling it will not make it safe to drink. There may be some special boiling water dispensers which will be marked as safe for consumption.

Health

Changes to your health. When you first come to the UK, the food you eat, the weather and the change in routine can affect your health. Foods such as baked and fried food can result in you feeling heaty (yang), or if you eat too many cooling foods such as salads, your body may become too cool (yin). Getting the right balance between warming, cooling and neutral foods is important in a new environment, so being aware of which foods will balance your body is useful. Note that UK doctors or your non-Chinese friends may not understand this concept.

Your General Practitioner. Check www.gov.uk for up-to-date guidelines on whether your visa allows you to use the National Health Service (NHS). Register early with a local General Practitioner (GP), surgery or health centre, so you can use it if required. Your university can provide a list of services in your area. Contact one to arrange registration and find out what documentation they need to see. Your GP is usually your first point of contact for illnesses not requiring emergency treatment. You can also speak to your GP for matters relating to mental health, such as anxiety, depression or stress. They can treat you by providing advice, referring you to specialists, or by prescriptions for medicine which you need to pay for. Take your prescription to a pharmacy or chemist where they will dispense the medicine. If further exploration is required you will be referred to a specialist hospital department and, depending on the urgency, this can take a few days or up to a few months if it's non-urgent. If you have an issue and it is outside of working hours, you can still call your surgery or health centre as their answerphone message will direct you.

Private medical insurance. You may decide to take out private medical insurance in China or the UK where they may be able to cover you whilst you study in the UK. It's important to ensure the policy you decide to take covers you for what you need.

Pharmacy or chemist. If you feel unwell and it isn't serious, you can visit your local pharmacy or chemist where a registered pharmacist can either prescribe over-the-counter medicines, or signpost you to further services such as your GP or hospital emergency services.

NHS service 111. For minor illnesses you can look online or telephone the 24-hour NHS service by dialling 111 where an operator will direct you to further services or advise you accordingly. Different countries in the UK may have different telephone numbers, so familiarise yourself with this according to where you study.

Emergency services. For immediate accident and emergency situations you can call 999 and the operator will ask if you need fire, police or ambulance. Tell them which service you require, for example, if you need an ambulance they will transfer you to a trained operator for advice. You can call this number on behalf of someone else, too. It's useful to find out where your closest Accident & Emergency (A&E) is and their opening times so you are prepared in case of need. Waiting times for A&E departments are often long and can be up to several hours depending on demand.

Dentists. Once you have registered with your GP and have your NHS medical number, you can register with a dentist. You can also register as a private patient at a dentist as they often accept both NHS and private patients. Similar to GP surgeries, some dentists have catchment areas, so you may need to live within it to register. You will need to pay for dental treatment, but NHS dental treatment is cheaper than private.

Opticians. You can use any optician in the UK and they usually have an appointment service, but some larger chains offer walk-in services. You will need to pay for the services, frames, lenses, contact lenses and other related products.

Weather

Four seasons in one day. As you start university during the autumn, you can experience all sorts of weather patterns which can happen all in one day. It's not unusual for days to start off rainy and cold, then for the sun to shine and it to feel very warm. Use weather apps to see what to expect for the day but be prepared for all weather as it can be unpredictable. Students suggest wearing layers you can remove and add as temperatures vary throughout the day, and to have hats, scarves, gloves, raincoats and waterproof shoes. A student asked me why she didn't see many local people using umbrellas. Generally, people in the UK don't use umbrellas to shield the sun, and when it's raining it's often too windy to use an umbrella. A waterproof coat is essential and if you can get a windproof one, it will help keep you warm from the wind.

Weather talk. One thing in particular that amused one student about British people was that she noticed they often talked about the weather. This is true. Conversations can often start with, "Isn't it a lovely day?" or "It's miserable today." And these statements will almost always refer to the weather which can impact the way people feel.

Transportation and travelling

Walking. Many students feel there is a lot more walking compared to in China, as accommodation can be situated far from the main campus. Campuses can be big and spread out, so getting to and from lectures and workshops can take time. Universities have maps and offer tours to help you familiarise yourself with locations.

Buses. Buses are the most useful form of transportation students use at UK universities because they are cost-effective and connect between accommodation, campus and shops. Universities may have campus buses specifically for students with stops conveniently placed between different buildings.

Bicycles. One student told me he would never use a bicycle in China, but in the UK he saw many students using them and decided to get one to travel between lectures and his accommodation. He said he missed out on walking together with his friends so he used his bicycle between his accommodation and university, and then spent the day walking with his friends between lectures.

Taxis. Taxis can be expensive but a useful alternative when needed. For some companies you must sign up on their app and the cost of each journey is automatically charged to the payment card linked to the account. When travelling with a group, it's a good idea to split the cost of your journey amongst you and your friends at the time of travel, unless you don't mind paying for journeys. People may forget to repay you afterwards, and you may feel awkward reminding them and risk being out-of-pocket.

Cars. As a convenient option, some students get a car. Before you do so, consider parking facilities at your accommodation and on campus, and legal obligations such as a driving licence, road tax, car insurance, car servicing and MOT (Ministry of Transport) tests, etc. You will find up-to-date information on www.gov.uk.

Trains. Trains are a convenient way to travel between cities, and depending on your route, there may be a direct train or connecting trains. For rail travel, you may purchase a card which provides student discounts on travel. To purchase one, check at your local train station or www.railcard.co.uk. Booking in advance for a specific train at a specific time can sometimes be cheaper. Pre-booking a guaranteed seat reservation is useful at peak travel times.

Coaches. Coaches can take you all over the country. Depending on the destination you wish to go to, it can be a cheaper or more efficient option than using trains. However, it can sometimes take more time as they use the roads which are subject to traffic conditions. There are some cost-effective options available with different coach operators.

Tube or trams. Depending on your location, you may also have the option of using trains on the tube or trams. Check with the service operator in your location to see if you can get any student discounts.

Queues. Waiting your turn in queues is the norm in the UK. Many students comment on how orderly public transport is as people queue to get on buses and trains, and how they enjoy the organised and less stressful way of using public transport.

Local area. Before you arrive it's useful to find out about the city or town you will be in. You can explore places of interest or those with historical significance such as theatres, parks, museums or areas to go shopping or places to eat. This will prepare you for what your location has to offer you.

Trips to other places. You can also extend your research to look at cities or places that interest you around the UK or even further. Depending on your interests, there are lots of places to visit and explore. As you research this you will discover more about each area that will add to your knowledge of the UK.

Finances

Bank accounts. Depending on the type of visa you have, you may be able to open a local UK bank account to provide more flexibility when managing your finances in the UK. If you don't get a UK bank account, you will consistently be charged fees for currency conversion and additional charges when you use your card to spend money or withdraw cash in the UK. If you work part-time, your employer will want to pay wages into a UK bank account. The major banks will be at your international student introductory week or Freshers' Week where you can book appointments to open an account. They may offer various enticements to persuade you, but don't get too influenced by this. Research and compare what you may use such as international transfers costs, the branch location (some are on campus), and products you need such as current account, savings account, debit and credit cards. Find out what documentation is required by visiting the bank's website and the British Bankers' Association. It's useful to bring some British pounds for the first few weeks before your bank account is set up, but make sure you comply and check www.gov.uk for amounts you can bring and what you need to declare.

Budgeting. Budgeting can be new to students and it is essential to manage finances properly from the start, otherwise you may run out of money too early. Allocate money accordingly to potential costs such as accommodation, books, bills, food, transportation, laundry, socialising, shopping, etc. Some find it useful to assign the lump sum of money on a termly, monthly or weekly basis to ensure all expenses are covered. In shared accommodation with shared bills, agree how bills will be paid, perhaps nominating one person to be responsible and others to commit to paying a regular contribution on time. One student told me she bought a luxury backpack at the beginning of the year and didn't realise how much it impacted her budget until the final term when she didn't have enough money left. Too embarrassed to tell her parents, she got a part-time job to help with her expenses. She enjoyed working, but would have preferred having more time for her dissertation. With hindsight she said she should have started her part-time job in the first term or not bought the expensive backpack.

Mobile phones. Mobile phone bills can get quite expensive and it's a good idea to look at the UK contracts available from different companies. They have different contract packages depending on your needs, such as the amount of data or calls you need.

Television Licence. If you are going to have a television in the UK, or access certain services from your mobile tablet, PC or laptop, you need a Television Licence otherwise you can be fined. They can be purchased online and you can check the TV licensing website to see if you need one.

Student discounts. Retail stores both online and on the high street often offer students discounts. There are online apps you can download and you can purchase cards such as the National Union of Students' TOTUM card.

Socialising

Clubs and societies. During Freshers' Week there will be lots of activities, clubs and societies to join, and everyone is looking to make new friends. It may seem extremely chaotic and feel overwhelming with so many events to attend. Advice from former students is to attend as many as you sensibly can and try things you may not usually be interested in. That way you can pick and choose what you want to continue with and you will find different types of friends along the way.

Pubs. A student who was in a flat with UK students found it challenging as they spoke so quickly and she couldn't keep up with conversations. They were extremely welcoming and invited her to their social events which mainly consisted of "going down the pub". Many UK students enjoy socialising at the pub compared to many Chinese students who may go to a restaurant or coffee shop. Pub culture is a part of UK life and it's a place for students to relax over a drink. Pubs offer a range of alcoholic and non-alcoholic drinks as well as food. You may find the pub outings fun, and if you don't, you can always invite them for a meal or coffee instead.

Nightclubs. Students who enjoy music and dancing enjoy socialising at nightclubs. These are usually situated in larger cities and towns. Your local Student Union will have music events and this is a great chance to meet other students.

Summary – The importance of settling in

Settling in well is important to provide you with a strong foundation for your UK university life. You know there will be some key cultural differences in the UK compared with life in China and preparing for them will help you settle in. By adapting to the new culture, without losing your own authenticity and cultural identity, you can benefit from having the best of both worlds. If you find yourself struggling to settle in, or feel isolated, upset or depressed, you can refer to your personal tutor or university's well-being services. There are online tools with information to support you such as self-help guides and understanding well-being staff who you can confidentially talk to. Settling into UK university life is not easy and it's important to get support or help early on to address any issues you may encounter.

Chapter 3

DIVERSE CIRCLES OF FRIENDS

Li Jing came to the UK excited to meet new friends from all over the world. When she arrived at her halls, she found most of the other students were from China. This surprised yet comforted her as she quickly made good friends with them. They joined Chinese society and began exploring the local area discovering all the places they could get their home comforts, especially food and drinks like bubble tea.

She thought she'd make different friends when her course started. However, she found most students at the business school were also from China. There were a few that weren't and they stuck together. She made the effort to speak with them and asked to join the group on a project for one of the modules. Although she found it hard to keep up with their conversation at times, she got to know them better as they spent lots of time working together.

During her year at university, most of what Li Jing did was within her Chinese community. When she was with her Chinese friends, it was

*comfortable and easy. But she also enjoyed being
with her project friends and after the project was
over, they still met up with each other by having
their lunch together sometimes.*

Through no fault of their own, students from China can
sometimes find themselves in Li Jing's situation. Many UK
universities now recruit the majority of international students
from China, housing them together in international halls to
help them settle in. Given that many Chinese students choose
to study business-related courses, business schools have a
large proportion of Chinese students. For other disciplines or
subjects, the proportions of Chinese students are lower and so
have a more diverse representation of students.

It's also understandable and natural for students to congregate
together with people from home. It's comfortable and important to
have Chinese friends because they can be your immediate support
network. But it's also as beneficial to have other friends from
diverse backgrounds to improve your English fluency, learn about
different cultures, and explore different interests. This will help
contribute to your personal growth and development, enabling you
to understand people from different countries and cultures.

Some Chinese students can initially feel disappointed as they
expect to have a multicultural experience and develop friends
from the UK and other countries. Although it may seem hard, it
is definitely something that can be achieved as there are many
ways to expand your circles of friends. The best and most effective
time to develop broad friendship groups is as soon as you start

university. Everyone is extremely friendly during the first few weeks, introducing themselves to one another, and almost everyone is nervous about making new friends, regardless of where they are from. Some students say they initially felt a little shy approaching non-Chinese students, but then found them generally to be friendly. If you come across someone who is unfriendly, move on as there will be plenty of others who are a better fit for you.

Tips on friendship etiquette in the UK

Smile or say hello to other students. It is not customary to smile at people you do not know, or to start a conversation with a complete stranger in China. However, in the UK, giving a little eye contact, smiling or saying hello to strangers is normal in everyday life. A simple act of smiling and saying hello is a great way to be friendly and start a conversation. Whether you are in a queue for a lecture or waiting in line for your coffee, smile and start a conversation about the weather or how long the queue is or just ask them how they are. This is not the time to get into deep and personal conversations, keep the topics light. If you see someone you don't know but recognise from your course or clubs you attend, it's also nice to acknowledge them by smiling and saying hello.

Friendship culture. It doesn't take long for Chinese people to become friends and talk about everything, including some very personal topics such as money, family and personal circumstances. In the UK, it can be more reserved at first as friendships form, and what may be deemed as acceptable conversation in China may not be in the UK, and vice versa. Therefore, general cultural differences will arise when it comes to making friendships with non-Chinese students. There may be an initial period when you are both getting to know each other to see whether you will click as friends; during this time it's not advisable to ask personal questions. The conversation may be quite superficial, sticking to safe topics such as where you come from, what course you are studying, where you live, which social events you go to, interests and hobbies, food, travel, etc. As friendships develop over time, conversations may start to get more personal, talking about family, feelings, aspirations, etc.

Most students want a diverse range of friends. The majority of students want to make friends from all over the world when they are at university. They are no different to Chinese students, so they will have friends who are similar to them, but will have and want to expand their circles to experience and learn about other people and cultures, too. One of the benefits of being in the UK is that it is a truly multicultural society.

Acquaintances. Acquaintances may be people you don't know a lot about, but you know enough about them to say hello and have a conversation with. These are often people on your course or who you meet at a club or society, who you don't spend a lot of time with. There may be potential for acquaintances to grow into closer friendships. You may find you develop lots of acquaintances and a few close friends.

Best of both cultures. Being authentic to yourself and acknowledging what you are comfortable with and what you want to explore are important. Trying out and adopting some elements of the UK culture will enhance your understanding of other cultures. There will be some aspects you enjoy and others you won't.

Ideas to expand your circles of friends

Follow your Student Union. Use social media apps such as Twitter, Instagram, Facebook, etc. to follow your Student Union to keep up to date with events and other information. You can then decide which events you want to attend to meet more people. Local UK students are heavily involved with their Student Union, so there will be lots of opportunities to meet them.

Get involved with your Student Union. Your Student Union always looks for volunteers, especially at the beginning of the academic year or for open days for prospective students. By volunteering, you will meet a mixture of UK and other international students.

Join clubs and societies you are interested in. Freshers' Week is the main time when clubs and societies try to recruit students. Joining these clubs and societies is a great chance to get to know like-minded people with similar interests. You could take a more active role in a club or society such as being on their committee or organising events. Even if you have an interest in something more unusual, there's probably a club or society for it, and if there isn't, you can set one up yourself as it's likely there will be other students also interested. One Chinese student loved everything Spanish and wanted to join the Spanish Society. Initially he was worried it was just for Spanish people, but they were extremely welcoming. We all love it when someone is interested in our culture and country. He made good friends from all over the world and improved his Spanish and English language speaking skills.

Join clubs and societies you may not be interested in. This is an interesting challenge, because this requires you to open yourself up to new experiences and interests. In doing so, you will meet students who you may not come across in your usual course of life. Many universities have over a hundred clubs and societies to suit students with a broad range of interests, hobbies and passions. Chances are you will find something new and, although it may not interest you initially, you may surprise yourself and love it.

Get involved in the community. If you have a religion, you can find and attend a local faith congregation which are always welcoming. You can find information about this online. Local volunteering services provide great opportunities to meet other people, not just students. Your university will have volunteering information online, or you can just search online for local volunteering opportunities.

Maximise group work opportunities. During modules or workshops, if you have the opportunity to work in groups or have group projects, choose to be in a group with a diverse range of students. This will provide experience of working with students who are different to you in terms of their opinions and ways of working. You will spend study time together learning to be flexible in the way you work with each other, and in doing so, these acquaintances may turn into good friends.

Attend networking opportunities. Universities organise events for students to get to know one another throughout the year. Both the Student Union and your school or faculty will do this, so take advantage of these events as a way to meet new people. Going by yourself may feel a little difficult and not within your comfort zone. However, if you go on your own, it's far easier to approach people and for them to approach you. A good tip is to introduce yourself to someone else who is on their own as it's likely they will welcome the opportunity to meet you.

Become a module representative or campus ambassador. These are positions of responsibility where you can support other students, and at the same time they will get to know you. You will also develop your leadership, communication and interpersonal skills to support your career development.

Summary – The importance of having diverse circles of friends

The comfort of having your circle of Chinese friends is extremely important to help you settle in and go through university life together in the UK as you share similar feelings and experiences. In addition to that, life at university in the UK brings you opportunities to make new friends and acquaintances with students from the UK and other countries. This diversity enables you to learn about people from different cultures and it can improve your interpersonal skills. A global mindset will help you with your career. A broad range of friends is the start of a broad network of people to keep in touch with for the rest of your life. You never know who you may be able to help or who may be able to help you in years to come.

Chapter 4

STUDYING IN THE UK

Liu Yang was a top student in China and was excited to come to the UK for her undergraduate degree in Marketing. She began her course surprised there was no textbook for each module, and instead was provided with long reading lists. When she looked at buying the books she realised how expensive they were. This troubled her because she was used to having the textbooks, highlighting and memorising the relevant parts. She decided to borrow the library books and found most were only available online. She adapted her approach to using online books and was delighted to be able to save the book, highlight and add notes. She struggled to read everything, and found the citing and referencing guidelines confusing. She was disappointed to have not done as well as she had hoped in her first assignment.

She went to see her module tutor who said she had not demonstrate her understanding of key concepts, had significant omissions, and her citing and referencing was inconsistent. She worked with him to adapt her approach and he signposted her to useful workshops to help with different elements of her studies. This helped her understand and adapt her study approach to what she needed to do for future assignments. Although she didn't feel as confident as she did studying in China, she knew there were people to help her.

Studying in the UK is different to studying in China. Many students get a big shock when they realise that learning and studying as they did in China does not translate into successful grades in the UK. Studying long hours may not be enough to get you good grades in the UK. This chapter helps you understand the key areas different to studying in China and how to evolve the way in which you study in the UK. The Chinese education you have received over your formative years provides a solid foundation to build on, but you must quickly adapt to the UK way of studying and learning in order to succeed in your UK studies.

What to take note of when studying in the UK
Relationships with lecturers and tutors. In China, you may be used to teachers being there whenever you need. UK lecturers and tutors are available to support you, but they may expect you to ask questions during classes or save them for your group or one-to-one tutorial sessions. Some allow you to drop in during the school day, but make sure you know what your tutors permit. You can expect to have different specialist tutors for each module. If you do a dissertation or thesis you will be provided with a specific

tutor to work with and have regular contact with them. It will usually be your responsibility to arrange meetings with them.

Personal tutor. You will be assigned a personal tutor who you can go to for any pastoral-related issues such as personal problems you may have. They will be able to support or signpost you to other relevant services such as the well-being team. As a minimum you should have termly tutorials with them, and if you need them in between tutorials their support is available, just contact them. Your personal tutor will get to know you well and you can ask if you can use them as a reference for jobs in the future.

Self-directed learning. In China teachers provide, teach and direct you to the information you require. At UK universities, they guide you, but expect self-directive learning where you manage your learning yourself. This is a more flexible approach that Chinese students and many UK and international students may not be used to. At a UK university you will be provided with the topics and some of the information which you use as a baseline to build on and read around in your own study time. This encourages you to do a large amount of self-learning through the core and extension reading lists provided. You may not be given textbooks for each module because you are expected to read a broad range of literature, drawing on different opinions to inform your own rationalised and argued opinions. You will also be expected to have your own opinions, to challenge and to reason the rationale of why you may think in an alternative way, or to build on what has already been written by others. Depending on the topic or the type of work you are asked to do, you can even come up with your own ideas which have not been thought of before, but make sure you base it on research or justify why and where your conclusions have been derived from. This way of studying can feel a little isolating at first, but speak to your tutors if you have any worries, as they will support you with your learning.

Blended learning. Universities may offer both face-to-face and virtual (online) learning. Virtual learning uses a combination of digital technology and platforms to deliver content. Ensure you are familiar with what your university uses and dial in a little earlier to ensure you are on time if it is delivered live. The following are the types of ways in which you will experience your learning at university, which could be provided either face to face or virtually.

- **Lectures.** Lectures cater to many students so you may be in a lecture hall or room with hundreds of others, or watching together on a virtual platform. It is essential that you take note of what the lecturer talks about, especially as they will direct you to other sources to explore further information. There is no need to note down every word, but understanding what is being taught to inform further research and learning is important. Note whether the lecturer welcomes or asks for questions and whether they allow questions at the end before you line up to ask, as they may be trying to get to their next appointment. If the lecture is delivered virtually, there may be an opportunity to ask questions using the chat functionality or by emailing your lecturer later.

- **Workshops.** These can also be quite large in size with many other students. A specialist presents key topics so you can gain deeper knowledge and understanding. Workshops provide opportunities for more interaction through discussions or asking questions, and group work is often involved where you work with other students. These opportunities are useful to develop the skills needed during job assessments when you may be assessed in group exercises.

- **Tutorials.** These are usually even smaller sizes than workshops and you may have a regular group of students to work with. Use these opportunities to practise sharing, discussing and debating your ideas with others. You may be asked to work in groups on projects, and you can use these situations to practise leading or working as part of a team, examples you can use during the job application process for your CV or during interviews. Learning how to work with different characters and personality types helps develop good interpersonal skills which are essential when you interact with interviewers, assessors or other candidates when applying for jobs and in the workplace.

- **Personal tutorials.** Use these to work with your tutor on things personal to you such as academic or pastoral issues. You must be proactive in booking these meetings and it's a chance to develop a good relationship with them.

Follow guidelines for each type of assessment. There will be clear marking guidelines on what's required to achieve the marks you aim for on each assignment. First-class grades of over 70% are usually only given to the top students for outstanding work. Marks can be deducted for going under or over the word count tolerances, and any additional words will not be considered even if it is the best part of your assignment. In addition to the usual assignments, essays or exams, there may be group work with presentations.

Reading lists. Reading lists will be provided to you for each module by the module leader such as the main lecturer or tutor. These lists will be available via the portal your university uses, and consist of a combination of books, journals, articles and web pages. These are now almost always accessible online via your university library or other libraries you will have access to as a student. In China you may be used to having textbooks for each subject, and you can ask your module leader if there is a particular one they recommend for you to purchase. However, these can be quite expensive. Most will be available to download online. Your university library will also provide support on how to use the library and learning services; they can help you borrow literature from other libraries and they may have a few hard print copies you can borrow if you prefer. Take note of what your lecturer or tutor suggests you read, as they may signpost you to a particular chapter, so you do not need to read the whole book.

Citing and referencing. Careful citing and referencing is important to prevent accidental plagiarism. Different universities follow different referencing styles and your university will have information about this online to familiarise yourself with. Self-plagiarism, where work from your own previous assignments is recycled, copied or resubmitted, is also not permitted. But if it helps demonstrate or build on new learning in your new assignments and it is properly cited and referenced, this is allowed. If in doubt, check with your tutor.

Summary – Studying in the UK

Studying methods in the UK are quite different to what you are used to in China and this can result in many students feeling confused, frustrated and isolated. Being prepared for this and learning how to adapt to this different way of learning and studying early on will help you understand what you need to do to continue to get the grades you want. Adhering to simple guidelines such as word count or formatting is important, as you can lose marks for these simple mistakes. Make sure you read what you've been advised to read on the core list and some of the extension list. Additional study workshops are useful to provide guidance on topics such as reading, writing assignments and dissertations, or constructing and giving presentations. You can also seek guidance from personal tutors or subject tutors and lecturers when you need to.

The first four chapters in Part 1 focused on how you can make the most of your university life in the UK to help you settle in and thrive. You may notice that much of what is shared is basic, yet so important to prepare you for your journey. The indirect learning you'll encounter through your experiences will contribute to your personal growth and development in the UK.

Part 2 shows how you can develop the skills, knowledge and experience to prepare you for your career. Whether you plan to apply for a job in China, the UK or the rest of the world, or want to set up your own business, your time at university provides a wealth of opportunities to capitalise on to help you stand out.

Part 2
CAREER PREPARATION

Chapter 5

MORE THAN GRADES AND CERTIFICATES

As a top student, Li Wei was always studious, spending all his time studying and focused on getting the best grades he could. His English proficiency was excellent, so he transitioned into his studies easier than some of his classmates. The UK teaching style was hard for him to follow at first, as his lecturers and tutors taught differently to those in China. But he listened to their guidance, read the core and extended reading lists, and attended all the additional academic and study support workshops. He signed up to everything he could to get certificates for his CV, spent all his time studying and consistently attained first-class grades in his work. The only time he took a break from his studies was to run three times a week, sometimes up to 10 miles at once, as he aimed to do a marathon one day.

He rarely went out with flatmates or classmates, and although he did chat to them, he never got to know them well as conversations were short and superficial. When he cooked in the kitchen he did this quickly, eating in his room so he could study whilst he ate. He also learned to batch cook so he only had to heat up his food, which meant he spent even less time in the communal kitchen. Li Wei never felt lonely as he was used to studying all the time in China.

At the start of his final year he applied for graduate roles to over 15 companies, including the main accounting firms, consulting firms and investment banks. To his disappointment he was only shortlisted for one graduate role, only to be rejected at the telephone interview stage. He asked for feedback and was told his excellent grades meant they had no doubt he could learn to do the technical elements of the role, but they felt he may struggle with other important elements required such as soft skills of time-management, teamworking, relationship and stakeholder management and customer focus, as he did not demonstrate examples of this during the interview. They were also looking for rounded people who demonstrated passions or interests other than studying or work. Li Wei was annoyed with himself for not having the soft skills they wanted and also for not telling them of his passion for running when he was asked what he did in his spare time. He had told them he had no spare time because he studied hard. He thought employers only wanted hard-working employees totally dedicated to the company at all times, but in fact this demonstrated poor time-management.

Li Wei achieved a first-class degree and went back to China and successfully gained an internship at a corporate organisation. But he wished he had also focused on developing a range of soft skills at university which would have enabled him to gain a permanent graduate position earlier.

Excellent grades matter and certificates are important to demonstrate certain levels of capability. However, there are many students with excellent grades and certificates. Great grades without anything else will be perceived as one-dimensional. To stand out from the crowd of other candidates who have great grades and certificates, you must build a broad range of skills, knowledge and experience. This can be gained through academic, extra-curricular activities and work experience. By doing this, you are preparing for your career. Regardless of whether you plan to apply for jobs or want to set up your own business, it is important to start developing what you need so you are ready to either demonstrate them during a job application process or use them when you set up a business.

HOW TO ENHANCE YOUR SKILLS, KNOWLEDGE AND EXPERIENCE

Find a passion or develop an interest

If you don't have interests, hobbies or passions, university is the perfect time to develop these. You may wonder how this links to your career. A student once refused to include his love of table tennis on his CV which we were reviewing for a job application. He was captain and school champion, represented the school at events, and coached younger students at summer camp. His aim was a consulting role in London and he was adamant his CV should only show academic qualifications and certificates. We discussed the transferable skills gained from table tennis, such as leadership, teamwork, influencing, presenting, and how this demonstrated dedication and determination, and that the voluntary coaching was a type of work experience. A way to stand out is to have a passion for something not related to study or work. This shows recruiters you are more than just someone who can do the technical elements of a job, and you can successfully balance other things. It also makes you memorable. Just imagine how many similar applications they see. Something different can make you stand out.

Some companies ask for presentations as part of the recruitment process. I've heard of an investment bank asking candidates to present 20 minutes on something they are passionate about which is not academic or work-related. When people talk about something they are truly passionate about, it is evident. You can then weave in what the recruiter wants such as the competencies they are looking for or how you align to the company's values.

Developing or having an interest in something is not only fun, but also good for your well-being. It can be anything you like, whether it is sports-related like football, activity-related such as visiting cities across the UK, or just something you enjoy like singing or drinking different teas. The important thing is to enjoy it and you may even find like-minded people, as there may be a club or society in your area of interest.

Play sports or exercise

In the UK there are different things to try which may not be as common or accessible as in China. For example, if you enjoy walking, there will be rambling club with trips to picturesque UK locations. You could try American football or lacrosse. There will be sports teams for most sports at your university, so someone like the table tennis student could join the university team, play non-competitively or help coach other members. It's a chance to get to know more students and there will be a social element such as Christmas parties, events and trips around the country when playing against other university teams. Whilst applying for jobs, it's good to include sports in your interests section, highlighting your proficiency and mention positions of responsibility – for example, if you have coached or organised events. In an interview a student mentioned she enjoyed learning to row on the river but didn't have upper body strength and went to the gym to improve. Coincidentally the interviewer loved the gym and suggested some core strength-building exercises. This not only demonstrated her self-awareness in being able to identify her development areas and how she looked at alternative ways to improve, but it also helped build good rapport with the interviewer and made her memorable.

Join any club or society you may be interested in

In Chapter 3, we touched on this as a great way to make friends. Your university will have a broad range of clubs and societies, including those which are academic or industry related, sports, community, performing arts and media, cultural and country, to name a few. Once you are in a club or society, you may wish to hold a position of responsibility to develop skills such as team working, organising, influencing, leading, etc. By taking a proactive interest, you may have the opportunity to shape the strategic direction of the club or society, develop relationships with people in your industry and support other students with similar interests. Use these opportunities to develop skills relevant to jobs you are interested in or to learn skills required to run a business.

Join a club or society in your subject area

This may seem obvious, but students from China seldom join clubs or societies in their own subject area or industry they wish to pursue a career in. If you study law join the law society or debating society, if you study languages, join the relevant language society, and so on. It helps demonstrate your passion for your subject area which deepens your dedication to your chosen career field. These societies are often sponsored or have ties with employers and alumni providing opportunities to engage with them. You will also meet like-minded students. Some students feel socialising together may not be a great idea because they are your competition, but most students support, encourage and wish each other well with their careers. Another important factor is that the people you meet here are the start of your network.

GET WORK EXPERIENCE

As an international student there will be visa restrictions on how much you can work during and after university in the UK. You can find up-to-date regulations by visiting www.gov.uk or your university's website, or by contacting the international team. Work provides a way to earn income and improve your English fluency. It's also a chance to meet people and gives opportunities to develop relevant and transferable skills, knowledge and experience to get you career-ready. You'll get an idea of what it is like to work in a particular industry or role in the UK, which also enhances your ability to think globally. There are number of different types of work experience options you can consider.

Internships

Many students are keen to gain internship experience because they think this is the only work experience worth doing. Internships are a great form of work experience, but extremely competitive to secure because there are not many places available and many students apply for them. Companies usually provide internships during the summer months. If you are an undergraduate student, you must apply during the autumn term before your final year. For postgraduate students, be aware most internships take place over

July and August when you may still be in full-time study doing your dissertation, which means your visa may restrict the number of hours you can work. If you are able to secure an internship, use this opportunity to demonstrate your value to the employer, learn and engage with the work, and take it as seriously as you would a permanent job. Companies sometimes use internships as an opportunity to see how students perform and their potential to fit in with their company. They can use this as a way to shortlist and recruit students. Some students have been offered full time roles following successful internships. Likewise, internships provide students with a way to test whether they will enjoy working within a company or industry.

Part-time jobs

Part-time jobs come in different forms and choosing something suitable depends on what you want to get out of it and the number of hours per week you can work within government regulations. Getting a part-time job in something similar to what you aim to do when you leave university can be challenging because companies rarely look for part-time staff whose main focus is their studies. Students often think it's only worth doing work experience if it is relevant to the industry they want to have a career in, for example, working in an accounting firm if they want to be an accountant. Yes, it would be useful if you can do this. However, if you can't get this type of work, other types of part-time work can also help you develop transferable skills to aid your career development.

Let's work this through with a common job students want to apply for – a consulting role. If you are unable to secure an internship or part-time job at a consulting firm, perhaps you can look at developing transferable skills in other ways. How relevant would working as a barista in a coffee shop be? You may think it is not relevant at all. Firstly, think about what essential skills consultants need. Perhaps these are: excellent communication skills, being a team player, problem-solving, creative thinking or being customer-focused. Here's how you could develop and evidence these skills whilst being a barista in a coffee shop:

- **Excellent communication skills.** Working with a line manager, colleagues and customers improves communication skills. Serving customers and listening to their needs to advise on the best solutions further demonstrates this.

- **Being a team player.** Working with colleagues, being supportive and flexible during shifts, and proactively performing tasks in addition to your job role can result in the whole team meeting their targets.

- **Problem-solving or creative thinking.** Opportunities to identify potential issues and learning how to solve them will arise. If there is a sudden shortage of a particular type of coffee during your shift, noticing this and diverting customers to other products or implementing robust processes to ensure coffee doesn't run out in the future are examples to demonstrate this.

- **Customer-focused.** Customer service is a key priority for a barista with lots of opportunities to demonstrate this.

If an employer was recruiting for the consultant role and they had two identical CVs in terms of academic achievement, but one demonstrated some relevant skills whilst working as a barista in a coffee shop part-time, and the other had no work experience at all, which do you think they would prefer?

When choosing a part-time job, be mindful of what you want to gain from it and how it can help you develop the gaps in skills, knowledge and experience to enhance your career prospects. Your university will often have a list of part-time job opportunities available in your area and some may be conveniently on campus. You can search online for part-time jobs in the area you wish to work in, or go in person to ask if they are recruiting.

Voluntary work

Another way to gain work experience is by volunteering, as it is seen as an altruistic trait because you sacrifice time to support others. You can volunteer at university, in your community or with national organisations. Your university will have links and partnerships with various organisations looking for volunteers, and this is often shown on their website. Many students have volunteered in China, so don't forget to include the skills and experience you gained relevant to any roles you may apply for. Here are some examples of types of volunteering you can consider:

Student-led volunteering. You can volunteer for activities, groups, clubs or societies within your Guild of Students or Student Union. You can gain experience in activities such as open days, being a student representative, a member of a student committees, organising events, etc. Your university will usually have a web page on this or you can contact your Student Guild or Student Union representatives for opportunities.

University department volunteering. Sometimes your faculty, departments or schools at university look for volunteers. This can include research, mentoring or providing other types of support to junior students. It's a great way of supporting other students, as well as your faculty or department. Ensure your tutors know what you are looking for and let them know you are willing to support them.

One-off volunteering. If you don't want to regularly commit to volunteering, there may be one-off opportunities to get involved in. This could be anything from gardening work for a local residential home, through to supporting an open day for potential students. These opportunities can be found through university and the local council where volunteers may be required to support a big event.

Community volunteering. You can get involved in your local community and there are lots of flexible opportunities to do this, such as residential homes for older people who often welcome volunteers to talk to and keep residents company which will develop your communication skills. You can give as little or as much time as you can, depending on your other commitments. The student I mentioned in Chapter 1 who volunteered at a library did it for a morning a week for three months. He initially wanted to improve his spoken English fluency, but there were other benefits gained from working there. He asked his manager for more responsibilities in addition to his task of meeting and greeting the public. As he was doing a marketing degree, he volunteered to promote a reading event planned for later that year, using it as an opportunity to apply some of the theory from his modules. This was a great example to demonstrate being proactive, creative, taking the lead and putting theory into practice when it came to him applying for marketing roles.

National volunteering. There are opportunities to support nationwide charities where you can organise events to raise money and awareness for a charity which enable you to develop skills such as organisation, influencing and customer focus skills. You could choose charities and organisations that align to your interests. For example, if you love dogs and miss your dogs at home, perhaps you can volunteer at your local dog rescue centre.

Research

It is useful to do thorough research to help you decide which types of industries or companies you may want to work in. This knowledge helps you interact with potential employers as you will be more prepared and able to talk to them about their industry and company. If you are interested in building a business in a particular industry, researching businesses already in your field is essential market research. There is a wealth of Labour Market Information (LMI) available, but try to focus on the more recent information to ensure it's up to date. Your university careers service will also have information to help. Most is available online, and information is now also provided virtually via webinars or online conferences.

Industry or employer events

These are available face to face or virtually, and are usually provided in collaboration with your university. They are events where industry experts and employers share key insight into their sectors and companies, which can provide an idea of what it's like to have a career there. You can also follow specific industries or companies on social media to engage and keep in touch with them.

Industry or company specific news

Keep up to date with current affairs and news related to the industries and companies you are interested in. This will provide you with broader insight to ensure you come across as well-informed during the job application process or help you develop your business ideas. It's useful to learn which industries are thriving or contracting due to different reasons such as advancements in technology, changes in consumer behaviour, or the economic or political climate.

Professional bodies

Professional body websites are useful to understand the current issues present in the sector you are interested in. They often provide networking events or virtual webinars you can sign up for to attend. This is a great way to network and learn more about what's relevant in that industry.

Job market

Keep up-to-date with what's available in the industries you are interested in, to understand where the emerging jobs are based by industry or location or where there is intense competition. This can help when choosing where to apply for jobs or help you see where business opportunities are. Your university careers service will have information about this.

Summary – Develop broader skills, knowledge and experience early on, because good grades and certificates are not enough

Good grades are important but many other students also have good grades, so you need to stand out from them by developing relevant and necessary skills, knowledge and experience that will excite your potential employers or give you a head start when developing your business. Stand out from the competition and start thinking about how you can choose activities to provide the relevant skills, knowledge and experience that match what employers or your business needs.

Joining clubs and societies provides you with other interesting things to talk about. A question often asked in interviews is: "What do you do in your spare time?" If you tell the interviewer you study in your spare time or you don't have any spare time because you study, then they are going to think you do not know how to manage your time effectively or are not a very interesting person for their team. Make sure you have an interest or passion in something, not only for your career journey, but for your own well-being and personal life.

Any work experience can be useful to help develop the skills you need to get a job or develop your business. You can consider internships, part-time jobs, voluntary work and positions of responsibility as they all provide real-life learning experiences to share during the recruitment process or learning for your business. Applying for jobs is not just about simply listing your work experience on your CV. It's about pulling out examples of skills and successes relevant to the job you apply for.

Researching organisations and their industries will give you a head start when applying for jobs or developing your business. Potential employers want to be assured of your interest in working for them and why you want to work for them. Your research provides valuable sources of information to demonstrate throughout the recruitment process when it is relevant. It will also help you to surface new types of work or business ideas you may be interested in or help you to determine what type of career you want.

Chapter 6

HAVE A CAREER PLAN

Zhang Min always wanted to be an accountant. Her father and uncle were accountants with their own business in China. She was strong at mathematics, extremely meticulous and organised, and felt the profession was perfect for her. Her parents encouraged her to study accounting and gain employment in the UK before returning to China to help the family business. She studied hard on her BSc in Accounting and Finance with a plan to apply to an accountancy firm for an internship in her second year, and then a graduate placement in her final year. She scored excellent grades at the end of her first year, but was unable to secure an internship. She also scored excellent grades in her second year, but was unable to get past the online application stage for a graduate role. When she went to her university careers service to seek help, they noted that her CV did not demonstrate the soft skills the roles she applied for expected. She went back to China to work in the family business, but wished she had gained some other experience before she did this so that she could add more value to the family business from working in other accounting firms.

Liu Wei did not know what he wanted to study and his parents suggested he go into finance and then decide whether to be a banker, consultant or perhaps something else. He had no pressure other than to go to university and get his degree. During this time he thought he'd like to work in the UK and applied for jobs in a broad range of industries from investment banking to retail graduate jobs. He applied to over 50 jobs but did not get shortlisted. He completed his undergraduate degree in finance with no job to go to, so his parents suggested he continue with a postgraduate degree in international finance. During the autumn term, he applied for similar UK roles as before, but still did not get any further in the application process. Upon completion of his studies he returned to China disheartened that he did not have a job and still did not know what he wanted.

Li Min was always thinking about business ideas and had a dream to set up a fusion-style restaurant or boutique hotel in her home town, Fenghuang. She didn't know where to start so she chose an international business degree to provide her with knowledge she thought she needed. Whilst in the

UK she decided to work part-time at a hotel as a waitress in the restaurant. There she developed her English fluency, customer focus and teamworking skills, and built up good resilience working under pressure. But most importantly, she got to know other colleagues whilst on her breaks in the staffroom. She learned about the positives and negatives about their jobs, and had the chance to interact with a broad range of people of different ages and backgrounds. She realised she needed to gain more hospitality experience to enable her to continue to build the knowledge, skills and experience to start to realise her dream. After graduation she returned to China and applied for internships at international hotels.

Some students know exactly what they want to do and have a clear idea of how to get there. Some students may be going down a path but aren't sure whether they want a career in the field in which they are studying. Then there are some students who do not know what type of career they wish to pursue.

You may be expected to follow a certain pathway because your parents or relatives expect it, or have responsibilities where you feel obliged to follow a certain path, such as working in a family business or following the profession of your parents. If this is the case and you are comfortable to follow this route, there is still a lot you can do to prepare for your career through developing the relevant skills, knowledge and experience. If you have other ideas or wish to find alternative career paths, you can speak to the careers team at university, who will help you to think creatively about how you can meet your needs together with any other obligations you may have.

Whether you think you want a particular job or want to set up your own business, the important thing to remember is your career will be fluid and that nothing has to be forever. Throughout your career you can switch from employment to self-employment and back, between companies or industries, and across different jobs and professions. What's important is learning from each step you take to find out what you are good at and what you enjoy.

Having a career plan helps make the most of your time at university. A career plan can be either a rough idea or a clear goal of what you may want to achieve, where you are now and the actions you need to undertake to get there. It can always be flexible, where the end goal and actions change as you discover more and progress. Students who know what they definitely want to do can have a more linear plan with clear actions on what must be achieved to get there. Depending on your own preferences, you may wish to develop an action plan to help you keep on track, or you may just mentally note your plan of what you wish to do.

THINGS TO CONSIDER WHEN CAREER PLANNING

Increase your self-awareness

Self-awareness is about knowing the different aspects of yourself such as your traits, behaviours and feelings. Some argue that having too much self-awareness can limit growth by preventing you from doing things or staying within your comfort zone, or it can limit you from trying new or different things. But having an initial level of self-awareness can help you understand why you may react in certain ways and use this understanding to challenge yourself to achieve even more. Spending some time thinking about what your values and beliefs are is a useful start. These will often stem from your parents and culture, but these can also be things that you truly believe in and have thought through yourself.

You may then like to think about what your strengths and areas of development are. You will then begin to realise why you are better at some things than others. Noting your interests and dislikes is a useful exercise to do as well. You may find you will often be much more energised and better at doing things you like. The things you don't like may drain you. You can cross-reference your likes and dislikes against your values and beliefs, strengths and development areas. This will help you start to see a picture of yourself and realise who you are.

Psychometric tools are useful and your university careers service can signpost you to some, and there are good free online resources available, too. Examples such as personality or strengths tests help you analyse what your values, beliefs, traits, strengths or weaknesses are. Personality tests can help suggest careers suitable to particular traits you have. It's important to take the results of all psychometric tests as just a source of information and to use them to complement other information sources. Don't be restricted by what they may tell you, as you know what is best for you. Some employers use a combination of psychometric profiling tests as part of their recruitment process to shortlist the types of people they think can fit within the teams they are recruiting into.

Explore and research different careers

If you are a student who doesn't really know what you want to do, now is the perfect time to start exploring the different careers and pathways. Learning through different experiences helps you find out more about what you may or may not like to do. Your university careers service may offer events where you can have opportunities to meet a broad range of employers.

Fairs. Whether fairs are called graduate fairs, job fairs or recruitment fairs, they are all similar as there will be employers ready to talk to students about their companies and available roles. Stands are often hosted by recent graduates who work there or employees who can tell you about the process of applying and what it is like to work in that company. They are great opportunities to network and showcase what you can do. Employers may look out for potential talented students to invite to apply, so have a CV with you, just in case they ask you for one. There will be different types of employers including local businesses and Small and Medium-sized Enterprises (SMEs) that you may not be aware of. Some universities organise events with employers from China which may be hosted at different universities, so it's a great opportunity to visit other places. Even if you are an entrepreneur, these events will be useful as you may decide to work for a short period in a company to gain experience before setting up your business or you can use it as market research. Part of career development is about exploring a diverse range of opportunities as you never know what you may find interesting, and it helps you narrow down your options. You can use it as a way to network with people in the company, by thanking them and highlighting what you found useful either in person, via email or on LinkedIn after the event. There is also a lot of labour market information available online such as careers sites offering information about different industries and types of jobs.

Employer events. Your university often organises employer events where employers share information about the company, what it's like to work there and the opportunities and pathways available. These are also provided to try to persuade the best candidates to apply. Employer representatives range from alumni, human resources teams to specialist employees. These are very useful to attend, even if you don't think you have an interest in working in that company or industry you may come across some useful information for your career development.

Company visits. If you are particularly interested in a company or sector, you can look at whether they offer company visits or experience days. For companies that offer this, you can either contact them or look online under their graduate careers pages. Some universities may even offer these experiences if they have relationships with companies students are interested in, so check with your university careers team to see what opportunities may be available.

Timing – be prepared for the job application season

Whether you are applying for internships or graduate roles for after you finish university, it's important to be aware of the timing of the job application season. Start dates for UK graduate jobs usually start in September which means applications start a year before the job's start date. For jobs in China the recruitment seasons are autumn enrolment from September to November, and spring enrolment from February to May. Autumn enrolment is the main recruitment season with more opportunities available.

For postgraduate students, the time when you apply for jobs coincides with the time when you first come to university. You will have several conflicting areas of focus such as settling in or adapting to your studies, as mentioned earlier in this book. Thus, if you can prepare as much as you can before you come to the UK, you will get yourself into a better position to be able to apply successfully for jobs during the autumn term. Preparing a CV before you come to the UK will help identify gaps early on which you can start working on. It's useful to arrange to bring your CV to your university careers service as soon as possible, so they can help you learn how to tailor it for the roles you are interested in.

The earlier you apply, the better chance you have because some companies close application dates early if they are able to fill their quotas. Your university careers service may have information about key closing dates for job applications. You can also find this out through graduate careers websites or directly through the companies you want to apply for.

Exploring SMEs or other industries

A student once told me that a senior told him the best chance of getting a UK job was to go for an audit role in a Big 4 accounting firm. He said he was only going to apply to them because if he couldn't get one of these it was unlikely he would get any other. Your seniors can be a great source of advice. However, put it into context and look at other sources, too. Even if you have all the relevant skills, knowledge and experience and excellent academic qualifications required for the role, limiting yourself to just applying to four jobs at the most competitive companies could be risky.

Exploring what other SMEs may have is a good approach to take as well. Most students focus on initially applying to the usual larger corporate organisations such as corporate organisations in the UK or China. However, SMEs are often overlooked by students at this early stage and only looked at later when students may have been unsuccessful in being shortlisted for their first choice of jobs. SMEs often have a more personalised approach to recruitment as they won't have the same recruiting resources as larger companies who hire agencies or use their own recruitment departments. The SMEs may also follow different recruitment timelines and can close recruitment early if they find suitable candidates. To get a head start, apply to SME jobs early on together with when you apply to the large corporate jobs.

Write your CV early

Most students only think about their CV just before they apply for a job. Whether you are constructing a CV for a job in the UK, China or the rest of the world, the most important thing is to highlight the relevant skills, knowledge and experience that relate to the job you apply for. Try to start constructing your CV early, before you arrive at university, to identify any gaps you need to address. This could involve getting more work experience, developing hobbies or interests, or having positions of responsibility. If you leave writing your CV to just before you apply for a job, there won't be enough time for you to develop the relevant skills, knowledge or experience required to address any gaps.

Writing a great CV takes time and consideration, and it's likely it will take a few drafts to get it into a cohesive and engaging format. Depending on which country your CV is for, there may be some differences in what to include. For example, a CV for a job in China requires a photo, but a photo is not required in the UK. Seek guidance from your university careers service who will offer CV writing workshops, online support and individual support to help you construct a great CV. If you want the individual support, visit them early on, as their appointments can get fully booked up during the peak job application season.

Know what's required for the job

The most important thing to consider when applying for a particular job is what employers look for. Just like with your CV, research this early on by looking at the types of roles you want to apply for at the beginning of your time at university. Take note of what particular job role profiles ask for and assess this against your own skills, knowledge and experience. If you do this early, you can look at practical steps and actions to take during university to gain what's needed. This is a key part of the career planning process, and it's easier to manage if you start early and give yourself enough time to do this.

You can find details on job roles during the autumn term at least a year before you are due to apply. Your university careers service has lots of useful information and guidance on different industries and roles. These can sometimes include industry expert workshops, literature and examples of other students who have previously applied. They may even have alumni or employer links they can signpost you to.

Construct tailored CVs and cover letters for each job application

Using the same standard CV and cover letter to apply for every job is probably the most common mistake students make. Recruiters and employers spot this immediately. Tailor your CV and cover letter to each job. With hundreds if not thousands of applications for one job position, it's critical to stand out. It's important to have already built up the skills, knowledge and experience early on so that this can be transposed onto your CV. This is why it is essential to start preparing for applying for jobs early on.

- **CV.** Try to make it easy for the person reviewing your CV, because they may only look at your CV for between 6 and 12 seconds. Many companies use Applicant Tracking Systems where technology automatically screens your CV focusing on programmed criteria such as key words. Think about how you can use the key words they use in the role profile. For example, if they ask for excellent customer service experience, make sure you use the words "customer service", and demonstrate examples of how you have delivered excellent customer service and what the outcome was. It can take a while to tailor each CV to the job, sometimes a few hours or more if done properly.

- **Cover letter**. Cover letters are sometimes required by employers. They accompany your CV and can be used to help you stand out from other applicants. Do not repeat what you say in your CV, but use it to bring out your personality, why you want to work for the company, why you are interested in the role, and what you can bring to the company. Keep it short, no longer than one A4 side of paper and make sure it's relevant to the job. Do not use a standardised cover letter for all your job applications, but personalise and tailor it, as you would for your CV. For guidance, visit your university careers service as they are likely to have examples to guide you and may offer workshops or individual guidance.

Don't apply for too many jobs

When I first started working with students, I mentored a student who wanted help finding a job. She had applied to over 120 jobs and had not got to the next stage with any of the jobs. She couldn't understand why because she had listed lots of work experience. I was not surprised she had been rejected from them all. I was surprised she had continued to apply to so many jobs and not stopped to find out why she was not seeing any success. Her reason was because she accepted that she wasn't what they were looking for. She didn't know what sort of job she wanted, so she thought that the more she applied for, the more chance she would have of getting a job that might be suitable.

Applying for jobs is not like playing the lottery. With jobs, the only time you will have a better chance of getting through is if you demonstrate you have the relevant skills, knowledge and experience for the role or for the job. If you are using one standard CV and cover letter for a broad range of jobs, the chances of you getting through to the next stage are extremely slim, even if you do have the prerequisites and capability to do the job. If you have not demonstrated this, the employer will not know.

I worked with this student to identify what she may like to do, and she found three jobs in digital marketing and four jobs in events she wanted to apply for. She tailored each CV and cover letter to each job and company. They were all general marketing roles which asked for the similar core competencies, but they also asked for different things. Each job was with a different company which meant further tailoring. By choosing different examples from her previous skills, knowledge and experience that were most relevant to the particular job and company she applied to, she realised just how different each CV and cover letter was. She was delighted when she was shortlisted for two of the jobs.

Prepare for the job application process

Practising for the different elements of the job application process early on will ensure you are more prepared for when you get shortlisted for the various stages of the application process.

Interviews. Interviews can be conducted via telephone, video or in person. Some employers provide questions and ask for a video of you answering the questions which you can upload for them to review later. Some companies even use artificial intelligence to undertake and analyse video interviews to help shortlist candidates. This sophisticated technology can pick up what you say taking note of your tone of voice and facial expressions. Most ask questions related to the required competencies for the job, and your answers should demonstrate relevant evidence. Thus, preparing a bank of examples is important so you can choose the most relevant and best example for a particular question. Help your interviewer by answering in a clear and structured way. The STAR (Situation, Task, Action, and Result) approach is useful to organise your thoughts, and helps interviewers understand the Situation you are highlighting, the Task you undertook, the Action you took, and the Result of what you did. Providing examples of what you did by using "I" not "we" will help them see what you did, because they are interested in you, not what your team or company did. They will also be interested in the impact of what you did on your team, company or customers, so bring this in too. Your university careers service can provide typical roles or industry-specific questions to help you prepare, and may provide opportunities to do mock interviews.

Aptitude tests. These tests are used by employers to ensure potential candidates have the level of aptitude required for the role. They are used alongside psychometric tests to provide a rounded picture of the potential candidate. Aptitude tests can consist of verbal reasoning, numerical reasoning, abstract reasoning, inductive reasoning, logical reasoning, and personality tests. These are part of the recruitment process and can be either online or at an assessment centre. Your university careers service will be able to show you where you can find relevant practice tests.

Psychometric tests. These tests are used by employers to gain an insight into the mind, skills and personality of potential candidates. It provides a way to see if you fit with the role they are recruiting for and with the company. If your results don't align to what the employer wants, then you may not get through to the next stage of the recruitment process. You can practise these tests, but it's important to answer questions honestly because you can be asked the same question in different ways during the same test. This is not to catch you out but it is to ensure you are answering truthfully. Inconsistencies in results will be noticed by the employer.

Gamification. Some employers use gamification as part of their recruitment process, particularly larger corporate organisations such as those in accounting and consulting. These assessments consist of online virtual games usually about an industry challenge or a company-related quest. Throughout the game they may test aptitude, creative thinking and problem-solving skills. Your aim is to demonstrate your thinking process and approach to problems and situations under pressure. The best way to play is to focus, follow the instructions and play it honestly. No two games are the same, as it changes depending on how you play and different companies look for different requirements dependent on the role they recruit for. You can prepare for this by ensuring you have experience in critical thinking and problem-solving which you can develop through academic studies, work experience and working with others.

References. When applying for a job you will be asked for references at some point during the application process. There is no need to put references on your CV, save the valuable space for other information. When it comes to choosing your references, think about who knows you well enough. You may be asked to provide a specific type of reference such as an academic, professional or work, or personal reference, or a combination of any of those. Before you provide a reference, ask permission from the person you would like to provide your reference. Some students ask their personal tutor or an academic tutor who knows them well. For professional or work references you can ask managers who you have worked with, which is another reason why it is important to gain work experience whilst you are at university. For personal references choose someone who can demonstrate another angle of who you are, such as a family friend in a professional position in China. References are usually sought by employers as that final check to ensure you are credible and suitable for their company

Networking. Some define networking as meeting people who may be useful to know, or exchanging information or services to develop professional contacts to help with your career. I like to think of networking as simply the act of building relationships with other people. Too many people network with the sole aim of doing it for themselves so they can meet people to help with their career. This can be seen as a self-centred approach and feel like an awkward process which is why many people do not like doing it. But if you think about your network as simply being the people you know, it can be less daunting. You don't know if they can help you in the future or whether you can help them, but it's good to have a network just in case opportunities to help each other arise in the future. Start to build your network with the students on your course, your friends, tutors, alumni and keep building it as you go through life. An international tool for building this is LinkedIn which worldwide employers use. Your university careers service may have guidance to help you set up your own LinkedIn profile with tips on how to use it, and LinkedIn itself has information to guide you. My main tip when connecting with someone new, whether it is face to face or virtually, is that you introduce yourself and explain why you would like to connect. Practise your introduction and always try to find a mutual reason to build a relationship with someone.

Summary – A career plan will help you prepare for your career

A career plan is important to ensure you have an aim and actions to get you there. It doesn't have to be anything complicated. The simple plans are the most effective. If you plan early and properly, you can break down your actions into manageable chunks of activity that can be done in a timely manner. This will prevent you from missing any important workshops or key dates such as application deadlines. It allows you time to book in things such as individual meetings with your university careers service without having to miss out on these because you have left it too late.

Identify your Strengths (S), Weaknesses (W), Opportunities (O) and Threats (T) with a simple SWOT analysis on yourself as this can be useful to compare yourself against the potential role you wish to go for or the business you want to set up. This provides an idea of your gaps and where you can apply actions to address them. You may have come across SMART actions which are Specific, Measurable, Achievable, Realistic and Timely. If you can place some SMART actions within your plan, it will keep you on track and help you achieve what is required in a timely manner according to your goals.

Your university careers service can help you build your career plan and may have online tools to guide you or individual support.

Chapter 7

GET HELP

Before Wang Jing came to the UK, she had already received lots of emails about things such as her accommodation, courses, activities and careers. She read about her accommodation before she came and saved everything else for later. Once she was in the UK, the communications continued to come. She had been invited to several different workshops and events during the induction week and went to as many as she could, collecting all the leaflets and booklets that were handed out to read later. There was a lot of information to absorb, and she found it overwhelming and difficult to keep up. Her course started and she had to quickly turn her focus to her studies.

Halfway through her first term, she noticed a classmate carrying a canvas bag with a logo of a company she wanted to work for, and asked where he got it from. He told her of the careers fair he had attended a week earlier. She was annoyed she had missed the opportunity to meet with this company. She went back to the emails, leaflets and booklets in her room and found lots of information about the careers events that were being held throughout the term which included workshops on CV writing, assessment centres and information about individual support. She also noticed a communication advising of graduate jobs and their closing dates which were within the next month. She decided to visit the careers centre to book an appointment, but they were fully booked up. They showed her the workshops and online information that would also help with her CV and the rest of the application process. Although the workshops were useful, she had wished she had tried to get an appointment earlier to benefit from the personal support.

One of the key times to get help with your career is early on. You may be surprised to hear that few students actually seek professional help for their careers during university. Many students only realise what's available when they urgently need it, which can be too late, as job application closure dates come quickly. This is sometimes because students are not aware of the support available for them. When you come to university you will receive a large volume of communication from all the different university departments, as well as information sent to you from third parties. This is intended to help, but as most students are trying to settle into university life, they may not have time to read everything. Some keep information to read and absorb later, but as time goes by they forget or other more important things may need their attention, such as assignments or presentations.

What support is available?

There are no services that can guarantee you will secure your perfect job or that you will develop a successful business. The responsibility for your career development is your own and only you can do what's needed to prepare for your career to get you where you want to. However, there are a number of support services and people who can help you with your career journey. I recommend you use a combination of what works best for you.

University Careers Services

UK universities provide careers services for their students, and depending on your university, there are varying levels of careers services available. This is the most important service you should use to help prepare for your career. The service is included as part of your course fees, and as you are already paying for it, it makes sense to use it. Many students do not use them for various reasons. Some are not aware the service is available or are so focused on their studies that they are not thinking about preparing for their career. Others may lack the confidence to visit the careers service or may be overwhelmed with the amount of careers information available. Some have said they have visited them too late, when no appointments are available or useful workshops have already taken place.

Having explored many of the careers services offered by UK universities, most provide an extremely comprehensive range of services to support every element of your career preparation and planning. Some can be accessed online before you arrive, so I highly recommend you familiarise yourself with what is available at your university so you can plan how to make use of these resources as soon as you arrive.

Due to the large volume of students, your university careers service is likely to provide generic support to cater for all students. There are some universities who provide support for specific departments or for international students. Universities with a high proportion of students from China may offer further tailored support such as CV tips for jobs in China and the UK, and careers fairs with Chinese employers. Some universities may have Chinese career practitioners on hand to support. However, this is not always available and any career practitioner can provide you with a great service. You will find them all extremely welcoming and you can be totally honest and open with them when talking through any career-related situation.

The services universities provide include practical support to help you through the job application process which can consist of:

- Developing tailored CVs and cover letters
- Online applications
- Psychometric test practice such as verbal reasoning, numerical reasoning, personality profiling and situational judgment tests
- Interview preparation in person, video or telephone, with sample questions
- Assessment centre preparation including group exercises, presentations and role play

There may also be some specific provision for career planning, with the level of personal guidance and support varying across universities. You may be offered individual one-to-one appointments ranging from 10 to 60 minutes, depending on your careers service. These are useful if you do not know what you would like to do or require guidance to achieve your goals. Universities can link you up with alumni who are a good source of information and support when it comes to your whole career journey. They may have mentoring schemes where you can be allocated to someone in the industry who can provide guidance or support to your specific area as they have direct expertise and experience.

Universities have strong links with employers and often organise careers fairs, company visits, company and industry talks or workshops and networking events where you can get to know more about roles, companies or industries, and meet potential employers. These events are often in the autumn term, so look out for them or contact your careers service to see when they are available so you don't miss them. They are a great way for you to explore and research what you would like to do and start developing ties with potential companies you may want to apply to. Some universities even offer projects to prepare you for the working world where you can gain practical experience. Look at what your university offers so that you are ready to apply for opportunities or schedule in events so you don't miss out on these informative and valuable opportunities.

Private Careers Services Companies

There are private careers services that specifically help Chinese students with the recruitment process. They often provide similar services to what universities offer. Some tailor and personalise the approach for you and provide industry experts to work with you. They usually focus on supporting you to get a specific job, so most students who use them know they want a job in a specific company or industry. They work with you on the application process which includes things such as constructing and writing your CV or cover letter. They may also provide information and help you practise interview techniques. This is the most expensive option and can cost up to thousands of pounds because the services are extremely personalised to you. If you choose to use these services, do your research to ensure they can provide what you expect before engaging them.

Family and friends

Traditionally students from China receive direct career guidance from parents, relatives and friends. These are useful sources of guidance especially if they are based on factual experience and information. Bear in mind their opinions may be based on their own experience of what they would like or not like you to do. They may also have broad networks of people that they can introduce to you to help with your career. Family and friends are a useful source of career guidance that you can use to complement other support services, such as your university careers service.

Alumni or other students

Alumni from your current and previous educational institutions are an important source of support when it comes to your career. They have been in your position before and have experiences which you can learn from and build on. Most are very willing to help their juniors and organise networks and events to support you. Your previous college or university and your current university will be able to provide you with details on how to link with them.

Do it yourself

This is the most common option students from China use and does not cost anything. However, it can take a lot of time navigating through what you need to do on your own. If you are self-motivated, resourceful and able to manage your time effectively, this is an excellent approach. I would recommend you also use the university careers services by picking the services, tools, information and events you may not have access to on your own. What you should be aware of is that you don't know what you don't know, so you may miss out on various services that could be crucial for your career journey. Some students prefer to do all their research online, and there is extensive information from many different websites and sources to support your career preparation. Your university will also have online careers support that will add value to your research.

Coaching

Employing a coach is a new concept for students and is a relatively recent development used in China. This is because coaching is often seen as a privilege that is exclusively provided to senior executives or employees who are considered top talent in organisations, or for business owners who hire coaches to help grow their businesses. A coach is impartial and will work with you to achieve whatever you want to focus on and aspire to. There are different types of coaching for example, career coaching focuses on how to develop and improve your career. If you would like to become more self-aware to help narrow down what sort of career you want, then a coach can work with you to do this. If you have any particular areas you wish to work on such as improving your confidence when speaking English, the coach can help you work through developing strategies or actions to improve that. If you want to set up a business, there are business coaches who can help you with that. Coaches help students focus on what really matters and what's important for them. Some students prefer individual support and the continuity of working together over a period of time.

Coaching can produce excellent results because it is tailored to you and works at your pace. The costs can vary and a good way to find one is via professional independent coaching bodies who have lists of registered coaches and career professionals where you can search for those specialising in students or Chinese students.

Which approach should you use?

As a coach myself, I would say that you should you use the approach that works best for you given your own specific needs and circumstances. Using a combination of approaches is useful, but foremost you should consider the way in which you like to work. For example, if you prefer to work alone in a self-directed or self-managed way, you can do it yourself and use the online university careers service to guide you. If you need constant support, guidance and encouragement, then visit your university careers service to see what they can offer or hire a coach to work with.

The reality is that many students can find the university services overwhelming and hard to navigate through, or are not even aware of them. The cost and intensity of using private career companies can put students off. Finding a suitable coach can be difficult and there is also a cost to this approach. This all results in students doing it themselves or with friends, trying to fit it in between studies, and submitting job applications driven by their deadlines, not realising what's required to prepare properly. This book has been written to help simplify the process by highlighting what you can do to prepare for your future career.

Summary – Start early and use your university careers service and anything else you may find useful

University careers services are keen to support students and offer a very broad range of career information, guidance and advice. Depending on your university, there will be a mixture of resources available such as one-to-one sessions and workshops which could be provided in person or virtually. The use of these services is not mandatory as part of your course. They are provided as additional support for career development. Students who prefer more support should approach their careers service early on to find out what is available to ensure workshops and events are accommodated into their timetable. Even for more self-directed and self-sufficient students, it's useful to see what is available at university to take advantage of networking opportunities or events with industry experts.

If you feel your university careers service does not offer you what you personally need, look to engage with the other services mentioned in this chapter. Do what is right for you and make sure you do this early on during your university life rather than leaving it to the end when you have other conflicting priorities such as final exams or dissertations to complete, or when deadlines have passed for job applications.

Chapter 8

BEING READY FOR YOUR CAREER

If you are someone who does not really know what they want to do for a job after university, or you don't get the job of your dreams, do not worry too much. Most people don't start their careers exactly as they thought they would. Many careers are non-linear and follow different pathways and routes. Some people start in a corporate career in a graduate placement role and then try different parts of the business, building transferable skills, knowledge and experience throughout their career to apply across businesses. Others start their careers in one job on a particular career path, only to find they do not enjoy it or it doesn't play to their particular strengths, personality or interests and will consequently move on to different jobs in other industries. Others may be entrepreneurs and set up their own business or businesses, they may even work as an employee first to develop the skills, knowledge and experience they need to grow their business ideas. Some don't just have one job and make up their income with a portfolio of work consisting of a combination of employed or freelance work. It's important to realise that there is not just one pathway. Be adaptable and flexible so that you can be open to exploring different routes along your career.

Start early and prepare. Being at university is the perfect time to be open to all the opportunities to learn and explore. Regardless of whether you want to get a job or you want to set up your own business, this chapter highlights what you need to prepare in order to be ready for the career ahead of you.

What you must do to get ready for your career

Qualifications
Qualifications are a way of demonstrating your aptitude and knowledge. They indicate to others that you have a certain level of knowledge. Qualifications are a great way of building up knowledge which you can apply in the workplace or the real world. It's useful to start applying what you learn such as during your work experience or any positions of responsibility you may hold at university. This will get you used to application of knowledge in the workplace.

Hard skills
Hard skills are work-related skills which you can specify and define, such as foreign languages, data entry or processing, computer technology of programming languages, finance skills like bookkeeping, or marketing skills. These can be gained through academic studies, self-study or courses, or during work experience. You can sometimes gain certificates as evidence of your capability and aptitude which you can use to demonstrate your hard skills. Hard skills are traditionally what people think of as the skills required for the world of

work because they are theoretical and can be applied in the workplace in a practical way.

Soft skills

Soft skills are skills which are highly transferable as they can be applied to different situations. These are the skills that are developed through practice, although there may be some courses or books where you can learn how to develop them, too. Soft skills such as communication, teamworking or collaboration, problem-solving or critical thinking, creative thinking, organisation and analytical skills, are highly transferable as you will use these in your daily life, both personal and professional. Developing a range of soft skills early before you arrive and whilst you are at university will help provide you with relevant skills for work. The great news is that you can develop these skills all the time by making opportunities to do this by using the experiences you have during your academic studies, work experience or extra-curricular activities.

Work experience

Work experience provides you with opportunities to develop the relevant skills, knowledge and experience required for your future career. It also provides you with opportunities to experience what it is like to work somewhere or in an industry which can help you learn what you like or do not like doing, and what you may be good at or not so good at. Chapter 5 gives some examples of the different types of work experience you can undertake during your time in the UK.

English fluency

English is a global language and is a useful additional skill to have for the workplace, as a lot of countries use English as the common language to do business in. People may expect that if you have a degree from the UK your English will be at a good level. Having the advantage of being able to communicate in English will stay with you throughout your career.

Getting a job – what employers want

It may surprise you to know that employers in the UK and China now look for similar attributes and competencies in their candidates. Employers shortlist based on academic qualifications, hard skills, soft skills and work experience. This means that they will look at how you have used your education, work experience and extra-curricular activities to develop and use skills they are looking for. Your chance to demonstrate this is throughout the job application process, meaning that it is essential you have already developed evidence of the skills they are looking for before you start the job application process. You must start as early as possible, regardless of whether you are still in China or in the UK. Those on undergraduate degrees have more time to do this. But for postgraduate students preparing an initial CV before arriving in the UK will be essential if you apply for UK jobs because the application process starts in the autumn term. If you are aiming for a job in China, you can use your postgraduate degree year to develop these skills. There are a number of different skills employers look for, but there is now an increasing importance on soft skills.

Qualifications. Employers use qualifications as a prerequisite to shortlist potential candidates. For CVs you can demonstrate this by including the name of your educational institution, academic qualifications, subject, and include grades or predicted grades together with dates. If you want to show you have particular expertise, you can also break down your degree to show what you learned and the outcomes from various modules or projects. Your qualifications may include certificates in certain hard skills which you can use to evidence your level of proficiency to employers. Your university careers service can show you how to do this.

Hard skills. You can look to develop the appropriate hard skills that are relevant to the jobs you apply for. For example, if an employer wants a candidate proficient in a particular programming language and you have experience of using that specific language, you should demonstrate this including what you have done and the outcome. If you have an idea of what type of job you want to have after university, you can look at the particular hard skills employers look for through researching the jobs they advertise early on. You can then identify the gaps you have and work on achieving the relevant skills required, so that you are ready when you come to applying for jobs.

Soft skills. Soft skills are now seen as another way to differentiate between potential candidates, and if you demonstrate you have these, you will stand out from the other candidates. Building up evidence of soft skills can help you demonstrate to employers that you can adapt and transition into their business with skills you can immediately use. These skills should be demonstrated using examples with evidence of how, why and what the result was. Your university careers service can help you understand how to do this.

Work experience. Employers do not just look at the company where you gained your work experience, but they also look at what you have achieved whilst you were there. If you are fortunate enough to get work experience in a related business to your chosen future job, then you must ensure you are able to provide examples of what you did there. Most students are unable to secure internships or part-time work at a related business in the field they want to work in, as there are very few of these roles available and the competition for them is high. Looking more broadly and gaining different types of work experience is important, too, as discussed in Chapter 5. You can use work experience to demonstrate the relevant hard and soft skills that are required for the job you apply for.

English fluency. Throughout the job application process in the UK, you will demonstrate your level of English language proficiency through writing, reading, listening and speaking. For UK jobs, it is essential that you can articulate yourself in a way that your employer understands, as a high level of English fluency is required to work in graduate jobs. If want a job in China where an international company is located or the company has international links, then this is going to be an advantage that can help you stand out. Having a UK degree alone will only help you stand out to a point, you must also demonstrate how good your English proficiency is.

Having a business

If you want to develop your own business, it is crucial to have a broad range of hard skills, soft skills and work experience to ensure you have the foundations to help you with your business. It can be argued that this is even more essential than if you were to go for a job in a company where you are expected to specialise in a particular area. You may have more time to develop the skills and experience you need as you have your own schedule for setting up your business. However, you may also decide that being employed first may help you develop the attributes and experience required for you to start your own business. Some students choose to work for smaller companies where they can get a broad range of experience of how businesses operate and are run. Other students may prefer to work in larger companies to learn about processes or gain an insight into international business. The path you take will depend on what your business idea is and the skills, knowledge and experience you have or need to develop.

Qualifications. Qualifications provide the theory you can use to help you set up and manage your business. Potential business partners may also look at this as a guide to see if they want to do business with you. Some of the most successful entrepreneurs do not have qualifications but have surrounded themselves with staff that do. It depends on the type of business owner you want to be. If you don't have certain knowledge from the qualifications you have gained, there is always the option to hire others who do to complement what you have.

Hard skills. If you know what skills are required for your particular business idea, you can ensure you work on these to match what's required. Or you may wish to know which skills you will need to employ talent in to complement the hard skills you already have. For those who are looking for funding for their business idea, you will need to demonstrate this as part of your business case to financial institutions or venture capitalists, to provide them with confidence that you have the hard skills required to make the business a success.

Soft skills. It is imperative to have soft skills if you want to have your own business. You will need to use your soft skills at a practical level as soon as you start developing your business. Examples are having great communication skills to articulate your idea to potential customers, or time-management skills to ensure you can effectively organise what needs to be done by yourself or with others. As you develop and grow your business you can work with or hire others who complement your strengths.

Work experience. Work experience provides opportunities for you to research what you need to know to run a successful business. If you decide to go straight into business, it may be useful to gain some work experience during university. Not only does it provide you with knowledge of what you may or may not enjoy or be good at, but it's also a great way of learning how different elements of businesses are run. For example, it will provide you with an opportunity to understand what it's like to be an employee, which will help you be a better leader for the staff you may have in the future.

English fluency. If you want to do international business, then having a good level of English fluency will help with business connections and potential customers. However, this will be less important if your focus is only the market in China. Even if at this stage you may not know the exact direction of where you want your business to go, it's a good idea to keep doors open for yourself and your business. Language proficiency is always an advantage in the global marketplace as it makes it easier for you to reach customers and business partners.

Attributes

Developing the right attributes is also important to prepare you for your future career. These will help you regardless of whether you are looking for employment or setting up your own business. Having your own unique selling points or personal brand differentiates you from others. It also provides you with what's needed for the challenges of developing your own business. Here are some of the types of attributes you should look to develop at university:

- **Resilience.** Resilience is about how you bounce back from setbacks or difficult situations. You may find that you are rejected from many job applications, or that beta testing of your business idea gives poor results, but how you learn, adapt and grow from this is what will make you more resilient and able to handle challenges better in the future.

- **Passion and motivation.** Being passionate about things will drive your motivation to accomplish challenges. Understanding what drives you will enable you to draw on this so that you can strive and attain your goals.

- **Initiative and proactivity.** Having initiative and being proactive are key attributes employers look for because they value different perspectives and people taking action without the need of being asked to do so beforehand. These are also key attributes to help if you want your own business, because progress will be your responsibility and driven by you.

- **Ownership and taking responsibility.** Whether you work for someone or for yourself, owning and taking responsibility for what you do is a key attribute required in the world of work. It will prove you can be trusted and accountable for work or projects.

- **Adaptability and agility.** Being adaptable and agile, especially in the current environment, are key skills needed to succeed. This enables you to be open to opportunities, even during times of turbulence or change.

- **Global mindset.** Having a global mindset is about having the ability to understand different cultures, countries and systems, and knowing how to use and apply this knowledge. By living in the UK you will have the benefit of gaining the experience of living abroad first hand. The opportunities to engage with other UK and international students will aid you in your understanding of different countries and cultures. This can be a great advantage for you.

Summary – The importance of using your university life to get career-ready

With millions of Chinese students graduating each year, preparing yourself so that you stand out from the competition is getting increasingly important. Whether you want to get a job in the UK, China or the rest of the world, it will be useful to prepare by getting career-ready to increase your chances of getting the quality graduate job you want. If you want to have your own business, starting to develop what you need during university will give you a head start with your business idea.

By going to the UK for university, you have started to differentiate yourself. But that alone isn't enough to prepare yourself for your career. Looking for and developing ways to gain further hard and soft skills that are relevant to your chosen field are important to give you an advantage. Work experience is a great way in which you can achieve this. Having interests, passions and hobbies which we touched on in previous chapters is also something that will help you stand out and be remembered.

Chapter 9

MORE USEFUL TIPS

ADVICE FROM CAREER PRACTITIONERS AND STUDENTS

"Embrace changes in your life and remind yourself of why you decided to study overseas when times are tough. Keep reflecting on your motivations, interests and skills while enjoying the process of learning. This journey is uniquely yours and you will shape your own future in the process.

Careers are non-linear and so your future is not predetermined. Find support from others and support others in the process. In times to come, you will look back at your own journey with joy, creating waves of victories for yourself to inspire others as well!"

Lisa Chow
Careers Consultant for ICMA Centre
Henley Business School, University of Reading

"1. Join a university society – *I joined Toastmaster, a public speaking club, where I trained to speak in English in public. I acquired knowledge such as body language, speaking ups and downs and how to catch the attention of an audience.*

2. Get involved in the local community – *I made great friends at church. We have great relationships as some were not only willing to chat with me when I suffered from homesickness, but also invited me to their homes. Thus, my life felt warmer and more interesting during that period.*

3. Participate in programmes offered by your careers centre – *My career centre ran a future leadership programme which has been very beneficial in preparing me for my career. It provided me with the chance to connect with entrepreneurs on projects, and trained us to communicate with colleagues and executives in a second language."*

Shao-an Wang
MSc Investments
University of Birmingham

"When my students are job hunting, I always ask them to think like a 'product manager'. A good product manager will have a good knowledge of their product and the customer's needs. This will allow them to highlight the selling points of their

product to meet the customer's requirements and to identify features they need to add. When job hunting, ask yourself the following questions:

- *What 'features' does the product (candidate) offer? Their knowledge, skills, experiences and personality.*
- *What are the needs of the customer (target company's vacancy requirements)?*
- *What is the gap between them? Can I fill those gaps within the limited time?*
- *How will I tailor my advertisement to the customer to stand out against the competition and secure my customer (dream job)?*

There is no 'perfectly matched' job or 'well-designed' thirty-year career path. The market is very dynamic and so are your knowledge and skills. Social media has existed for less than 20 years; ten years ago, artificial intelligence was more science fiction than a growing industry. The job title, function or industry may change but core skills are always in demand. Find your passion and keep on picking up new skills and experiences around it. You may not be able to predict your job title in five years' time, but you can carry on doing the tasks you like and are good at."

Xiaobei Wu
Careers Consultant
Imperial College Business School

"From my experience, networking events during the welcome week are very important as you can meet new friends there. Participating in events run by societies will help international students get involved in new campus life. Keep an eye on the school's career website, where there are lots of amazing activities and opportunities to visit big-name companies, talk to employers and learn about their candidate requirements."

Jin Zhao
MSc International Business
University of Birmingham

"My advice for prospective students is to take the rich opportunities available to you whilst you study in the UK, such as, improving your English language and cultural awareness. You can develop these skills by mixing outside of your own culture groups e.g. join a mixed student society, mix with peers outside of your culture in your classes and volunteer or work part time around your studies. Don't wait for opportunities to come to you, go out and find them. These skills are sought after by employers and will help you to stand out."

Lisa Donnelly
Careers Adviser
University of Birmingham

*"1. **Volunteer.** Join volunteer organisations as they link you to the working world and connect you with the local community, helping improve your English speaking skills by communicating with local people across cultures. I joined a local charity helping people with disabilities. I felt the warmth of home chatting with them, and my empathy and listening skills were nurtured – very beneficial to my professional coaching studies. The tip before choosing voluntary work is linking back to your major and future competencies required by your dream job. Choosing the right project experiences can be a huge endorsement in your job-hunting process.*

*2. **Get out of your 'shell'.** Many Chinese students don't like raising their hands in class to share opinions and rarely interact with non-Chinese classmates during breaks. One local student told me they appreciate and respect those who express themselves in class. I would suggest we try stepping out of our comfort zone and not always stay in the small social bubble with Chinese students. Asking other local or foreign students to have lunch together is worth a try.*

*3. **Leverage resources.** Overseas students pay high tuition fees and deserve to make use of educational resources. As well as courses, seminars, libraries and sports venues, professors are also resources.*

Stay in active contact with mentors, tutors or course directors and make the most of your tutorial time.

4. Goal Setting. Before departure to the UK, ask yourself what's the goal of your study period, dream you want to achieve, kind of a different person you want to be. Make a to-do list, step-by-step to realise your dreams, set up small milestones. It will definitely make you feel more fulfilled."

Lassie Chen
MA Career Development and Coaching Studies
University of Warwick

"Be a good friend to yourself.

Adapting to a new country, culture, and way of living is highly challenging. My first six months of living in the UK brought me a lot of tears. I had trouble understanding the native speakers (I still do sometimes), and I felt that I didn't fit in with the social activities. People around me all looked so confident and well prepared, but not me. All of this made me feel anxious and incompetent. The inside voice was telling me I wasn't good enough and gave me a hard time.

If you have noticed that judging voice inside of you as well, I'd like you to imagine that your best friend was in the same situation. What you would say to them? Gently try to switch the 'judging' voice into this 'best friend' voice. We often know how to be kind to others, but forgot how to be kind to ourselves.

Learn to be a good friend to yourself."

Nuo Xu

Career Coach

Warwick Business School

Useful resources

British Bankers' Association: www.bba.org.uk/publication/leaflets/international-students

British Council: www.britishcouncil.org

British Council in China: www.britishcouncil.cn

Career Development Institute: www.thecdi.net

Chinese Embassy London: www.chinese-embassy.org.uk

Coaching ST: www.coachingst.com

Government UK: www.gov.uk

Graduate Recruitment Bureau: www.grb.uk.com

Highfliers: www.highfliers.co.uk

LinkedIn: www.linkedin.com

National Union of Students: www.nus.org.uk

NHS: www.nhs.uk

NHS 111: www.111.nhs.uk

Prospects: www.prospects.ac.uk

Railcard: www.16-25railcard.co.uk

Targetjobs: www.targetjobs.co.uk

The Times Top 100 Graduate Employers:
www.top100graduateemployers.com

TOTUM card: www.totum.com

TV Licensing: www.tvlicensing.co.uk

UCAS: www.ucas.com

UK Council for International Student Affairs:
www.ukcisa.org.uk

Bibliography

Bandura, A. (1977) *Social learning theory*. Englewood Cliffs, NJ: Prentice Hall.

British Council (2018) *Employability in Focus, exploring employer perceptions of overseas graduates returning to China*, education-services.britishcouncil.org.

Cao, X. (2017) Enhancing the Employability of Chinese International Students: Identifying Achievements and Gaps in the Research Field, *Exchange: the Warwick Research Journal*, 5(1), pp77–89.

Chen, P.H. (2009) A Counseling Model for Self-Relation Coordination for Chinese Clients With Interpersonal Conflicts, *The Counseling Psychologist*, 37(7), pp. 987–1009.

Edwards, V. and Ran, A. (2006) *Meeting the needs of Chinese students in British Higher Education*, University of Reading.

Fan, W. and Leong, F. (2016) Introduction to the special issue: Career development and intervention in Chinese contexts, *Career Development Quarterly*; September 2016, Vol. 64 Issue 3, pp192–202.

Guile, D. and Griffiths, T. (2001) Learning through Work Experience, *Journal of Education and Work*, 14 (1), pp113–131.

Hao, D., Sun, V.J. & Yuen, M. (2015) Towards a model of career guidance and counselling for University Students in China, *Int J Adv Counselling* (2015) 37: 155.

Hawthorn, R., Kidd, J. M., Killeen, J., Law, B., and Watts, A. G., (1996) *Rethinking Careers Education and Guidance – Theory, Policy and Practice*, London: Routledge.

Hodkinson, P. (2009) Understanding career decision-making and progression: careership revisited, *Career research and development: the NICEC journal*, 21: pp4–17.

Huang, R., Turner, R. and Chen, Q. (2014) Chinese international students' perspective and strategies in preparing for their future employability, *Journal of Vocational Education & Training*, 66:2, pp175–193.

Illeris, K. (Ed.) (2009) *Contemporary theories of learning*, Abingdon: Routledge.

Inkson, K. (2007). *Understanding Careers: the Metaphors of Working Lives*, Thousand Oaks, CA: Sage.

Kolb, D. (1984) *Experiential learning: experience as the source of learning and development*, Englewood Cliffs, NJ: Prentice Hall.

Krumboltz, J.D. (2009) The happenstance learning theory, *Journal of career assessment,* 17(2): pp135–154.

Law, B. (1981) Community interaction: a 'mid-range' focus for theories of career development in young adults, *British journal of guidance and counselling*, 9 (2): pp142–158.

Leung, S. A., Hou, Z-J., Gati, I. and Li, X. (2010) Effects of

Parental Expectations and Cultural-Values Orientation on Career Decision-Making Difficulties of Chinese University Students, *Journal of Vocational Behavior,* v78 n1 pp142–158.

McQuaid, R.W. and Lindsey, C. (2005) The Concept of Employability, *Urban Studies*, 42 (2): pp197–219.

Mezirow, J. (2009) An overview on transformative learning, in K. Illeris (ed.) *Contemporary theories of learning*, Abingdon: Routledge.

Mok, K.H., Wen, Z. and Dale, R. (2016) Employability and mobility in the valorisation of higher education qualifications: the experiences and reflections of Chinese students and graduates, *Journal of Higher Educational Policy and Management*, 2016, Vol. 38, No. 3, pp264–281.

Patton, W. and McMahon, M. (2014) *Career development and systems theory: connecting theory and practice* (3rd edition) Rotterdam, Netherlands: Sense.

Reynolds, A. (2018) *Chinese Students in UK Further Education*, Routledge, Oxon. (eBook).

Rogers, C.R. (1994) *Freedom to learn*, New York, NY: Macmillan.

Simon, R.I., Dippo, D. & Schenke, A. (1991) *Learning work: a critical pedagogy of work education*, New York, NY: Bergin and Garvey.

Simpson, C. (2017) Language, relationships and skills in mixed-nationality active learning classrooms, *Studies in higher Education*, v42 n4 pp611–622.

Sun, V. J. and Yuen, M. (2012) Career Guidance and Counseling for University Students in China, *International Journal for the Advancement of Counselling,* 34(3), pp. 202–210.

Tomlinson, M. and Holmes, L. (2017) (eds) *Graduate Employability in Context: Theory, Research and Debate,* London: Palgrave Macmillan.

Tudor, T. R. (2018) 'Fully integrating academic advising with career coaching to increase student retention, graduation rates and future job satisfaction: An industry approach', *Industry and Higher Education,* 32(2), pp. 73–79.

Weiss, F., Klein, M. And Grauenhorst, T. (2014) The effects of work experience during higher education on labour market entry: learning by doing or an entry ticket?, *Work, Employment & Society,* 28(5), p. 788.

Zheng, W. (2017) Beyond cultural learning and preserving psychological well-being: Chinese international students' constructions of intercultural adjustment from an emotion management perspective, *Language and Intercultural Communication,* 17:1, pp9–25.

Zhang, W., Hu, X. and Pope, M. (2002) The Evolution of Career Guidance and Counseling in the People's Republic of China, *Career Development Quarterly,* 50(3), pp. 226–236.

Zhou, D. and Santos, A. (2007) Career decision-making difficulties of British and Chinese international university students, *British Journal of Guidance & Counselling,* 35(2), pp. 219–235.

Acknowledgements

This book has been developed with the support of many people. Firstly, a huge thank you to the hundreds of students from China I've had the pleasure of working with, particularly those who wanted to contribute directly into this book to support future students: Shao-an Wang, Jin Zhao (University of Birmingham); and Lassie Chen (University of Warwick).

There are many dedicated careers practitioners working across UK universities who have helped with the development of this book – too many to highlight, but thank you to everyone who spoke with me. A special thank you to Jayne Sharples for introducing me to the University of Birmingham where I must thank Julie Wainwright for the opportunity to work with undergraduates, and Tripp Martin who welcomed me to his team to work with postgraduates (thanks for writing the foreword to this book, too!). I also want to mention and thank the following people who share my passion and offered additional support: Lisa Donnelly (University of Birmingham); Alison Collins, Nuo Xu (University of Warwick); Kathryn Saunders, Barnaby Mollett (The London School of Economics and Political Science); and my fabulous beta readers Lisa Chow (Henley Business School), Yiyun Ling (University of Sheffield), Xiaobei Wu (Imperial

College Business School) and Xiao Ma (China Exchange).

As a new author, the guidance from publishing specialists has been instrumental in getting my thoughts into a finished book. Thank you to: my book buddy Helena Kim for your encouragement and advice; Morgan Gist MacDonald (Paper Raven Books) for your patience and getting me started; and Douglas Walker and Frances Prior-Reeves (Self-Publishing Partnership) for taking this book to print.

Finally, a massive thank you to my family: Paddy for watching over me and Lexie for being close by my side; my daughter Nicole for being a harsh and insightful book critic; my husband Soo Teck for supporting and indulging me with this project; and to my parents who have started supporting the next phase.

About the author

I'm Suzanna Geh Sun Tan and as you see from my name, I am Chinese. I was born and grew up in the UK, in a very traditional Chinese family with two younger brothers. Career guidance was provided by my parents. As with many Chinese parents they hoped I'd do medicine. However it was soon evident that I lacked the aptitude, and business was the next-best option. I went through university life without any thought for the career ahead of me. I finished my degree in June 1993, started looking for a job, but had missed the deadlines for the September graduate training programmes.

My mother said I could work at the family accounting business or find a job in Malaysia. The adventure of living abroad was exciting, so I went to Malaysia and got a stockbroking job. I returned to the UK after three years, worked at the family business and my father soon realised I didn't have the aptitude for accounting either. I spent the next two decades with Barclays in a variety of roles including marketing, business development and product management. As a senior manager I had additional responsibility for colleague development consisting of leadership training, career development projects, mentoring and coaching.

At 40 I finally realised what I loved doing - helping others with their careers. I had years of practical coaching experience, but no formal qualifications. It took another four years before I built the courage to resign. I went on to get professionally accredited as an executive coach with the Association for Coaching, achieved a Diploma in Coaching and a distinction in an MA in Career Development and Coaching Studies at the University of Warwick. It was there that a new interest was sparked.

I knew the UK was a popular destination for international students, but only whilst studying at university did I realise the sheer volume of students from China. Curious, I focused some of my studies researching their career development needs and found their experiences at UK universities fascinating. I also started providing them with career coaching and guidance. Key themes emerged in the areas of support they most needed. These were not just job-related, but centred on personal growth and career preparation.

There is so much help and support for students, but it can be overwhelming. This led me to develop this book where I hope to make it easier for new university students to navigate their way through UK university life. University is a big investment. So it makes sense to use the whole rounded learning experience to set yourself up for life, both personally and for your career.

Some people tell me I'm entrepreneurial, others say that I'm corporate through and through. Both have some truth. I now have a portfolio career doing a variety of different work. Apart from working with students, I manage my business coaching middle/ senior managers on their careers and leadership skills, support my husband with the family accounting firm, and manage a small property portfolio. I live in Birmingham (UK) with my husband, teenage daughter and dog, and I'm an aspiring vegan with a conflicting unhealthy obsession for handbags.